Writers at Work

The Essay

TEACHER'S MANUAL

Dorothy E. Zemach
Lynn Stafford-Yilmaz

CAMBRIDGE UNIVERSITY PRESS
Cambridge, New York, Melbourne, Madrid, Cape Town,
Singapore, São Paulo, Delhi, Mexico City

Cambridge University Press
The Edinburgh Building, Cambridge CB2 8RU, UK

Published in the United States of America by Cambridge University Press, New York

www.cambridge.org
Information on this title: www.cambridge.org/9780521693035

First published 2008

A catalogue record for this publication is available from the British Library

ISBN 978-0-521-69302-8 Student's book
ISBN 978-0-521-69303-5 Teacher's manual

ISBN 978-0-521-69303-5 Paperback

Table of Contents

Introduction

Audience

Writers at Work: The Essay is ideal for intermediate to high-intermediate ESL or EFL students who are ready to write fully developed essays with an introduction, body paragraphs, and a conclusion. This text is appropriate for adults and young adults, college and university students, high school students preparing to write at the college level, or anyone who wants to sharpen standard English writing skills for use in an academic or professional setting. It is also appropriate for native speakers of English who are developing their competence as independent writers in English.

Approach

Writers at Work: The Essay is organized around the writing process and guides students through this process in easy-to-follow steps. Numerous student sample essays, along with the presentation of clear organizational patterns, give students a helpful foundation to refer to in developing essays that are not only expressive and rich in content, but also clear and cohesive.

As you progress through *Writers at Work* with your students, you will undoubtedly enjoy seeing the students become engaged in the content and student-centered activities. For us, one of the greatest satisfactions in using *Writers at Work* is watching the students develop a warm, supportive camaraderie with one another, revealing how much they have connected with each other as partners in the learning process.

The writing tasks in this text focus on common organizational patterns and types of writing used in formal essay writing: explanatory, problem-solution, comparison-contrast, persuasive, and responding to a reading. All of the activities in a chapter relate to the particular pattern or type of writing. In this way, students are able to apply what they learn in their own writing. The final chapter prepares students to write timed essays such as they might encounter in classroom situations, in writing examinations, or when they apply to college or graduate school.

Writers at Work: The Essay makes it easy for you to serve as an effective guide or facilitator. Student-centered activities in the text imply that the students naturally take an active role in the learning process. But as the teacher, you always play the most vital role in any classroom situation. Your presence, your guidance, and your encouragement make the course ultimately successful for your students. You are the dynamic presence that inspires your students toward achievement.

Organization of the text

The book contains two major parts:

Essay Writing Basics

In this short introductory section, students review the basic conventions used by essay writers in English. They define an essay and learn how to follow standard formatting for an essay. They also study the types of essays in academic life. Students also focus on the importance of audience and on how to select a topic. Finally, they examine the writing process, not only as a process for writing, but also as a process for thinking and developing ideas.

Chapters 1–6

Each chapter opens with a page designed to stimulate students to think about the topic of the chapter and the type of writing they will be learning. Chapters are organized into five sections, each corresponding to a step in the writing process. (The final chapter, *Timed Essays*, follows a slightly different pattern.) These sections are described in the following notes.

Chapter structure

Each chapter has five sections:

I Getting Started

Students start out by looking at a graphic or statistical representation of a given topic. This information is designed to stimulate students' interest in the topic of the sample student essay. The sample essays are written by real ESL writing students. While they have been edited, the content remains true to what the students themselves originally wrote. It's a good idea for you to point out to your students that the sample essays don't represent an absolute standard that they must attain, but rather serve as a goal to work toward. After reading the sample essay, students work through a series of questions which focus attention on the structure and ideas in the essay. After answering these questions, students work to select a topic that they will write about in their own essay, generating ideas and working with peers to define their work.

II Preparing the First Draft

In this second section, students compose their thesis statement. They think about ways to organize their main ideas and they write their first drafts. Students are introduced to outlining as a tool for planning their first drafts. Information and activities throughout Section II assist the students in filling in their outlines. You can assign the first draft as a homework assignment.

III Revising Your Writing

Students learn about the key elements of good writing, practice checking and revising for these key elements in pieces of writing, and then apply these principles to the revisions of their drafts. In *Benefit from peer feedback*, students receive input for revising their drafts. This activity also gives students valuable practice in analysis as they analyze their partner's draft for revision. Of course, students are expected to make their own final decisions about the changes to make in their own drafts. Ideally, you can do Section III, *Revising Your Writing*, and Section IV, *Editing Your Writing*, on the same day.

IV Editing Your Writing

Students learn about selected aspects of grammar and style, do activities to practice editing pieces of writing, and then apply this grammar information to editing their drafts for accurate grammar and usage. Some instructors are in favor of peer editing for grammar, while others prefer to skip it or do it only from time to time. Omitting peer editing does not compromise the writing process, so you should do what works best with your class. You can assign writing the final draft as a homework assignment.

V Following Up

The first activity of this section, *Share your writing*, is to be done after students have written their final drafts, but before they turn them in to you. Here, through a variety of activities, students have the opportunity to read and enjoy each other's essays.

Each chapter ends with *Check your progress*. After students have gotten back their marked essays from you, they should fill out the *Progress Check*, a form that has them consider the strengths and weaknesses of their essays. The *Progress Check* will also help them see the improvements that they make and reflect on their writing throughout the course.

An Invitation to Write

We welcome your questions, comments, and suggestions. You can e-mail us at zemach@comcast.net. We look forward to hearing from you!

Warmest wishes,

Dorothy Zemach and Lynn Stafford-Yilmaz

Essay Writing Basics

In this introductory chapter, students will review or learn the definition and format of an academic essay in English. They will discuss the importance of defining the purpose for writing, of identifying your audience, and of choosing an appropriate topic. In addition, they will learn the stages of process writing and the importance of each one.

With your students, read the chapter introduction on page 1. Ask, *What is an essay?* Elicit answers from volunteers, but do not correct wrong answers at this point. If you like, write students' comments and definitions on the board, and leave them up while students work through Practice 1.

I WHAT IS AN ESSAY?

A Define an essay *page 2*

The purpose of this "quiz" is both for students to realize what they already know about essays and to learn the proper terms for the features of an essay. In addition, it serves as an icebreaker for students to get to know one another. For this reason, you may wish to have students do the exercise in small groups instead of pairs. The answers are intended to be obvious, but it is still a good idea to go over them with the whole class.

Answers

1 c	5 a	9 a
2 b	6 c	10 b
3 b	7 b	11 b
4 b	8 b	12 c

B Notice essay format *page 3*

Read through the information box, *Essay Format*, with your students by reading it aloud yourself, by calling on a volunteer to read it aloud, or by having students read it silently to themselves, raising their hands to show you when they are finished. Tell them that the gray boxes found throughout the book contain useful information. As you read this box, tell the class about specific preferences you have for the formats of their essays, including whether you will accept handwritten or only typed essays. Remind students that different instructors will have different requirements, and that they should always check with a new instructor if they are not sure what is required. The recommendations given here are standard to North American English academic essays.

Practice 1 *page 4*

After going through the directions, make sure that students understand that there are three body paragraphs to label and three topic sentences, so they will have to use the letters *a* and *n* three times each.

Answers

1 h	4 n	7 f	10 a	13 g	16 n
2 e	5 l	8 a	11 a	14 n	17 j
3 k	6 m	9 b	12 c	15 d	18 i

C Understand the purpose *page 6*

Read through the information box, *Purposes for Essays*, with your students. Explain that an essay assignment is usually some kind of a "test" for a student – of critical thinking, of the student's understanding of an issue raised in class, or of a student's ability to research. Clear writing and accurate language will help students successfully demonstrate their intellectual abilities.

Practice 2 *page 7*

Answers

1 b
2 a
3 a
4 c
5 c
6 b

II AUDIENCE AND TOPIC

A Identify your audience *page 8*

Read through the information box, *Audience*, with your students. Tell your students whom you consider their primary audience to be – you? Their classmates? Someone else? If you will have different audiences throughout your course, let them know that you will always tell them the audience in advance. If their audience is you and/or their classmates, point out that they will get to know more about the audience as the class progresses.

Practice 3 *pages 8–9*

Point out to students before they begin that there are several possible answers, depending on the focus a writer wants to take. However, some elements will more naturally lend themselves to some audiences.

Possible Answers

1 • People who have no knowledge about vegetarianism: b, any of the others
   • People who are concerned about the environment and health: a, c, d, i, j
   • People who are interested in world cultures: a, g, h
   • People who don't have much time for cooking or money for food: a, e, f
2 Answers will vary.

Practice 4 *page 9*

Answers

1 c
2 a
3 a
4 a
5 b

B Choose a topic *page 10*

Read through the information box, *Topic Selection*, with your students. Let students know if in general you will be assigning topics or letting them choose their own. Point out that while a personal interest in a topic makes the essay more interesting to write, there are other criteria that must be considered during topic selection. In this book, the criteria are pointed out in each chapter.

Practice 5 *page 10*

If you like, have pairs share some of their topics and write them on the board for the whole class to see. Point out that a great variety of topics can be drawn from a general idea.

Answers will vary.

III PROCESS

Practice 6 *page 11*

Read through the information box, *The Writing Process*, with your students. It's important that they understand that all successful writers follow this process, not just students.

Practice 6 draws an analogy between the process of writing and another artistic process. You may choose to solicit examples of other activities students know that follow a similar process; for example, planting a garden, planning and cooking a meal, arranging or decorating a room, and so on.

Answers

1 The artist gets ideas from her own life and from seeing other people's paintings.
2 She generates ideas for her painting by making some rough sketches.
3 She chooses the parts of her sketches she likes best and organizes them.
4 She paints the painting.
5 She shows the painting to her friends. They give their opinions and make some suggestions.
6 She makes some changes based on their comments.
7 She displays her painting.

Practice 7 *page 12*

Answers

a 4
b 7
c 3
d 2
e 1
f 6
g 5

Practice 8 *page 12*

Possible answer

A writer goes through several steps to create an essay. First comes choosing a topic from reading, talking to other people, listening to lectures, personal experience, and so on. Next comes brainstorming ideas onto paper and then organizing the notes. After writing the first draft, the writer gets some feedback from a reader, makes some changes and writes a second draft, and then hands in the final paper for others to read and enjoy.

Learn from writing *page 12*

Read through the information box, *Learning from Writing*, with your students. As your course progresses, share with your students examples of how you use writing in your own life; for example, to write reports, papers, and articles. Explain how you go through the various stages of the writing process and what you learn from your writing. This will help students see that the skills they learn and practice in this book will apply to their lives beyond the classroom.

Chapter 1 | Explanatory Essays

For Chapter 1, students will read and analyze a sample explanatory essay and then write a five-paragraph academic essay that explains the significance of a person, activity, or event in their lives. The chapter leads them through the steps of the writing process as they gather ideas, compose a thesis statement, organize their ideas into an outline, write a first draft, exchange and analyze drafts with a classmate, and then revise and edit their drafts to submit final polished essays. Students also learn and practice common transitions to help their writing flow smoothly and sound more sophisticated. They focus in this chapter on the introduction and conclusion, including different types of effective hooks, the placement of the thesis statement, and how to tie a conclusion back to the introduction. In the editing section students work on writing short but expressive essay titles, and they check their essays to make sure that their explanations are clear and complete. They learn to punctuate sentences correctly with the transitions presented in the earlier part of the chapter.

With your students, read the chapter introduction on page 13. Ask, *What people and events have been important in your life?* Call on volunteers to share answers or let students give answers in small groups. At this point, they do not need to go into detail about the people or the events; they are just bringing these ideas to mind.

GETTING STARTED

A Think about the sample essay topic *page 14*

Tell students that they are going to read a student's essay about her school years. In preparation, they will learn some vocabulary for talking about school and discuss general ideas related to the topic.

The chart shows information about the educational system in the United States. If it seems relevant or interesting, point out to students that grades are sometimes divided differently in different cities, depending on the population of the area. (For example, in some cities, elementary school comprises grades 1–6, students in grades 7–9 attend a junior high school, and high school is only three grades, 10–12.) Have students work in small groups to discuss the questions. Mix students from different countries or areas if possible. Call on volunteers to share information that surprised or interested them about their partners with the whole class.

B Read the sample essay *pages 15–16*

Read or have a student read aloud the focus question before students read the essay. They can jot down their ideas in the margins or on a separate piece of paper as they read. Have students nod or raise their hands to let you know when they are finished reading. Then have them briefly answer the focus question with a partner. As a class, discuss their answers.

If you wish, students can discuss these additional questions in small groups or as a class. Write the questions on the board.

 1 Do you think most students would learn the same lessons from boarding school? Why or why not?
 2 Do you think the writer could have learned the same lessons from a day school? Why or why not?
 3 What would be some benefits and challenges for you of attending boarding school?

C Notice the essay structure *page 16*

Read through the information box, *Explanatory Essays*, with your students. Emphasize that even an explanatory essay usually gives the writer's opinion or judgment about the topic; this opinion is usually the writer's reason for writing the essay.

Practice 1 *pages 16–17*

Have students answer the questions alone and then compare answers with a partner or group, or do the exercise in pairs. Ask students to mark the sample essay when directed with a pencil, not a pen, in case they need to change their answers. The task guides students to discover the essay's purpose, structure, and key features. Since these elements are important for each student's writing, go over answers with the whole class. Point out how the topic sentences of the body paragraphs are located in different places (at the end, in the middle, and at the beginning).

Answers

 1 b
 2 She believes that attending boarding school benefited her.
 3 Even though these things were not easy to learn, the lessons from my boarding school experience made me an independent woman and a productive member of society.
 4 c
 5 how to make true friends, obey rules, and return her parents' love
 6 Even now, the friends I made there are my treasures; However, I slowly learned that the rules of the school helped me to live easily and well; While staying at school, I learned to be thankful for my parents.
 7 c

D Select a topic page 17

Read through the information box, *Topics*, with your students. Point out that it's important to choose a good topic before going further with the writing process, if possible.

Practice 2 page 18

Have students work with partners to analyze the topics. Make sure they understand that most poor topics can be improved. Then have each pair join another to share their answers, or call on volunteers to share their answers with the whole class.

Answers will vary.

Your turn page 19

Remind students to choose a topic they are interested in. If students choose their own topics, make sure they show them to you before they begin the next section.

E Brainstorm page 19

Read through the information box, *Listing*, with your students. Emphasize that their purpose when brainstorming is to collect as many ideas as they can. They will evaluate their ideas later.

Practice 3 page 20

Have students work in pairs. One student can open the book to the essay, and the other student can open the book to the exercise. Point out to students that the list contains single words as well as short and long phrases.

Answers

Ideas not used: expensive for parents; best friend was Sachiko; classes were difficult; prepared me for college; class president; tennis team.

These ideas were not directly related to the writer's topic and opinion.

Your turn page 20

Give students five minutes to write. If they need more time, give them an additional five minutes. Tell them that since they will refer to their ideas in future classes, they should keep their lists.

F Discuss your ideas with others page 20

Have students take turns in a small group sharing their topics and brainstormed ideas. Other group members should ask questions to help the writer think of details or explanations. The writer should take notes on any new ideas that come up. If a group does not seem to be successful, exchange some of its members with a different group.

A Compose the thesis statement *page 21*

Read through the information box, *The Thesis Statement*, with your students. Point out that the thesis statement comes at the beginning of the essay, usually at the end of the introduction, and signals to the reader the topic and the writer's opinion. In academic writing, clarity is extremely important, and the thesis statement should clearly indicate the writer's position.

Practice 4 *page 22*

Have students explain why each "a" thesis is weaker. Make sure students see how the second "b" answer in each pair (items 1–2, 3–4, and 5–6) is a stronger thesis statement than the first "b" answer because it is more detailed.

Possible Answers

1 "a" doesn't name the topic (we assume that what the writer learned will be the topic) and is too broad; "b" specifies what the brother taught (how to be a better person)
2 "a" is broader than "b"; "b" specifies three aspects of being a better person
3 "a" isn't clear enough; "b" specifies why it was a great vacation (it changed the person)
4 "a" is broader than "b"; "b" specifies what the person realized (the value of an education)
5 "a" doesn't give the writer's opinion; "b" specifies how the person perceived the failure (as lucky)
6 "a" isn't as clear as "b"; "b" specifies in what way the failure was lucky (found a new career)

Practice 5 *page 22*

Students can do the exercise in pairs, or do it individually and then compare answers with a partner. Call on volunteers to read their revised thesis statements to the whole class, or write them on the board.

Answers will vary.

Your turn *page 23*

You may wish to model analyzing a thesis statement before students work in pairs. Call on a volunteer to write a thesis statement on the board. Go through the questions listed with the whole class. If the thesis statement is not strong, guide the student through a revision. Then have students work in pairs. Tell students they will be using the thesis statements for the essay, so they must keep a copy of it to bring to future classes.

B Edit your brainstorming *page 23*

Students should consider their thesis statements as they reread their lists of ideas. Remind students of the kinds of information the student writer of "Life Lessons from Boarding School" crossed out (ideas that did not directly support her thesis statement).

C Order ideas *page 23*

Read through the information box, *Emphatic Order*, with your students. Point out that it's easiest for a reader to remember the final idea in an essay, so many writers choose to put the most important idea last. Explain that ordering the importance of ideas is subjective, and there isn't necessarily a "right" order; in addition, sometimes a writer might not consider one idea to be more important than another. However, the writer should still consider which idea should be the final one the reader encounters.

Practice 6 *page 23*

Point out to students that the order they choose will depend on what points they consider the most important. Each student's answer may be different, but students need to explain why they have chosen a specific order.

Answers will vary.

Your turn *page 24*

Have students work in pairs. Remind them that the final decision about order is their own, and they do not need to follow the order their partners suggest. However, if partners choose a different order, they should discuss their reasons.

D Make an outline *page 24*

Read through the information box, *Outlining*, with your students. Sometimes students feel that outlining is more time-consuming than just beginning to write the first draft. Explain that a clear outline actually helps students write faster, because they will know which ideas to write when. It also prevents problems with organization that could cause significant rewriting later on.

Practice 7 *pages 24–25*

Point out to students that the ideas in the outline are worded slightly differently from the sentences that the student writer used; however, the ideas are the same.

Answers

Basic Outline

I.   INTRODUCTION: Thesis statement: I learned how to make true friends, obey rules, and return my parents' love.

II. I made friends with different kinds of people.

III. I learned why and how to obey rules.

IV. I was thankful for my parents' encouragement and tried to do my best.

V.   CONCLUSION: In boarding school, I learned that I could grow by facing challenges.

Practice 8 *page 25*

After students complete this exercise, have them compare the outlines in Practice 7 and Practice 8 and imagine writing an essay from each one. They should see that a writer working from the outline in Practice 8 would have an easier and faster time writing a first draft. If you like, you can show how each level of the outline is numbered or lettered in a different way; however, students should not worry too much about numbering or lettering, but rather concentrate on the ideas. They can simply indent to show further levels of detail. For further practice, have students outline another one of the body paragraphs in the same way, or have the whole class help you do it on the board.

Answers

A. 2. hobbies
B. 1. required patience and thoughtfulness
C. 1. a. being homesick; b. disliking certain classes

Your turn *page 26*

Encourage students to make a detailed outline, but if they don't feel ready, let them start with a more basic one. They can also add ideas to the outline as they discuss it with their groups.

E Use transitions *page 26*

Read through the information box, *Transitions*, with your students. Explain that combining sentences helps their writing sound more sophisticated and smooth. There are only seven coordinating conjunctions, and they connect sentences in the same way and are punctuated in the same way. Encourage students to remember the seven coordinating conjunctions. (They will learn the punctuation rules in Section IV).

Practice 9 *page 27*

Answers

1 so	3 so	5 but	7 In addition/so
2 yet	4 so	6 nor	8 for

Read through the information box, *Because and Therefore*, with your students. Point out that these are not coordinating conjunctions, and are used somewhat differently.

Practice 10 *page 27*

Point out to students that they need only circle the word *and* when it connects two clauses. For example, in these two sentences in the first paragraph, students would circle the following: *Those years were challenging and full of problems, but still, I gained a lot from them. After I graduated from elementary school, I left my family and went to live at a boarding school because my hometown was very far from my middle school.*

Answers

Paragraph 1: however, but, and, because, but
Paragraph 2: Therefore, However, so,
Paragraph 3: because, because, however, because, However, and, because, and, and, and
Paragraph 4: and, In addition, because, because, because, but, so
Paragraph 5: and, In addition

Practice 11 *pages 27–28*

Go over the directions together with students. Point out that they don't necessarily have to combine the two sentences into one sentence. A transition can join two sentences.

Possible answers

1 Professor Hayden gives a lot of homework. However, he is a popular instructor.
2 A part-time job teaches responsibility, and it gives you spending money.
3 My parents both worked when I was in school, so I had to learn to take care of myself.
4 Playing team sports is supposed to build cooperation and group spirit. However, I don't like feeling responsible for letting my team down if I make a mistake.
5 In the middle of seventh grade, my family moved to a new city. I was sad to leave my friends behind, but I quickly made new friends.
6 On Labor Day, people in the United States honor workers, so workers get a day off to rest on that day.
7 Learning a language is like playing a sport because you have to practice a lot in order to improve.
8 Learning new software applications will help me find a better job. Therefore, I'm going to take a class at the computer center.

Check that students have underlined transitions. Remind students to keep their body paragraphs with other pieces of the essays that they have written so far.

F Write an introduction *page 28*

Read through the information box, *The Structure of an Introduction,* with your students. Tell students that they will be examining the different parts of an introduction in more detail in this chapter and in subsequent chapters.

Practice 12 *pages 28–29*

Answers

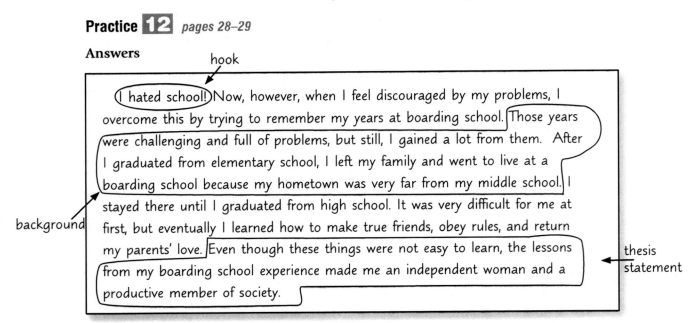

hook

I hated school! Now, however, when I feel discouraged by my problems, I overcome this by trying to remember my years at boarding school. Those years were challenging and full of problems, but still, I gained a lot from them. After I graduated from elementary school, I left my family and went to live at a boarding school because my hometown was very far from my middle school. I stayed there until I graduated from high school. It was very difficult for me at first, but eventually I learned how to make true friends, obey rules, and return my parents' love. Even though these things were not easy to learn, the lessons from my boarding school experience made me an independent woman and a productive member of society.

background

thesis statement

Read through the information box, *Hooks,* with your students. Point out that a hook can be the last thing that they write. Students should not fail to begin writing just because they cannot at first think of a catchy hook.

Practice 13 *page 30*

Possible answers

Hooks 3 and 5 are not effective; hooks 1, 2, 4, and 6 are effective. Students will have different favorites.

1 Effective: It is interesting and catchy.
2 Effective: It is interesting and imaginative.
3 Not effective: Hooks should not announce the topic of the essay in this fashion.
4 Effective: It uses questions to draw the reader in.
5 Not effective: It asks a question the reader might answer with "no" and then lose interest.
6 Effective: It begins with an interesting quotation.

Your turn *page 30*

Students may write more than three hooks if they can. Invite a few volunteers to read their favorite hooks.

G Write a conclusion *page 30*

Read through the information box, *The Conclusion*, with your students. Tell students that if they find they want to discuss an additional idea in their conclusion, they can go back and add that idea to their outline and body.

Practice 14 *page 31*

Answers

1 a, b, e

Practice 15 *page 31*

Answers

Conclusion 1 is the weakest, because it isn't detailed enough. Conclusion 3 is also weak because it adds new information.

Conclusion 2 is the strongest. It matches hook 2 from Practice 13.

Your turn *page 31*

Students do not have to tie their conclusions back to the hook, although if it's possible to do so, encourage them to try.

H Write the first draft *page 32*

Let students know that as they write their first drafts, they can make changes to the pieces they have already written, if they wish. However, they should not completely revise their thesis statements or outlines without checking with you first. Students can write their first drafts in class, or they can write or type them as homework.

III REVISING YOUR WRITING

A Benefit from peer feedback *pages 32–33*

Read through the information box, *Using and Giving Peer Feedback*, with your students. Make sure students understand that they are not grading their partner's paper, but rather responding to it. Tell them that it's just as important (if not more so!) to give positive, encouraging comments as it is to point out potential problems. In addition, tell students that a writer won't always agree with the comments from a peer reviewer, and that the writer is not obligated to change the paper based on the reviewer's comments. However, the writer should always consider the comments carefully.

Have students exchange papers with a partner. If you don't have an even number of students in your class, have one group of three exchange papers. Give students sufficient class time to read their partner's essay carefully. When both students in a pair have completed their feedback forms, they should go over the forms together, one at a time.

B Title your essay *page 34*

Read through the information box, *Titles*, with your students. Like the hook, the title does not need to be written before the rest of the essay, and in fact, is often written last.

Practice 16 *page 34*

Possible answers

Answers will vary. However, Title 1 could be considered too boring. Title 3 is definitely too long, and should not be a complete sentence. Title 6 could be considered too broad, although opinions will vary.

Your turn *page 34*

Have students check their title for correct capitalization.

C Critical thinking *page 35*

Read through the information box, *Revising*, with your students. Encourage students to read their essays out loud at home, either alone or to a friend, to hear their writing in a different way. They should consider each sentence. Is every sentence in the essay necessary? Is every necessary sentence present in the essay?

Practice 17 *page 35*

Students can also do this exercise in small groups.

Possible answers

1 The paragraph is trying to explain how hard the writer's brother works. However, the point is just repeated over and over in slightly different ways and is not truly explained. Some of the repetitive sentences should be deleted, and explanations and examples should be added.
2 The paragraph explains how the writer's brother set a good example. The explanation is clear and thorough.
3 The paragraph is trying to explain how the writer's brother is also the writer's friend. However, the sentences about other people's relationships with their brothers are not relevant and should be deleted. Explanations and examples should be added.

Your turn *page 35*

Have students check to make sure that their explanations are thorough. They can consider the feedback from their peer reviewers as well.

D Make revision decisions *page 36*

Students should consider their partner's comments and their own ideas.

E Write the second draft *page 36*

Students should use their notes to write the second draft. This can be done in class or as homework.

IV EDITING YOUR WRITING

A Punctuate transitions *page 36*

Read through the information box, *Punctuation with FANBOYS*, with your students. Point out that one reason students memorize these transitions together is because they are punctuated in the same way.

Practice 18 *pages 36–37*

Answers

1 My family hosted a foreign exchange student, so I wanted to study abroad, too.
2 I had to quit the team or improve my grades.
3 I couldn't follow what he was saying, for he was talking too quickly.
4 My father lost his job, yet he didn't become discouraged.
5 My parents told me I looked fine, but I had no confidence in my appearance.
6 My father found out I had told a lie and punished me for it.

Practice 19 *page 37*

Read through the information box, *Punctuation with Other Transitions*, with your students. Point out that while a comma is not required before *because* when it comes in the middle of a sentence, occasionally they will see a comma there when the sentence is very long. After completing Practice 19, for further practice, students can also go back and check the sentences they wrote in Practice 11 for correct punctuation.

Possible answers

1 Everybody liked my uncle because he was funny and kind.
2 Movies taught me a lot about far-off places. In addition, they taught me about different kinds of people.
3 I didn't have any experience, yet I wanted to find a job in sales.
4 Some computer games teach children how to think. Therefore, these games should be considered educational.
5 Because there have been many accidents at that intersection, the city should install a traffic light.
6 Many students study computer programming in college. However, there are not enough jobs for all of them.
7 I want to study French or German, so I can travel easily in Europe.

Practice 20 *page 38*

Answers

> A second advantage of attending a public school was meeting many different kinds of people. The children in my neighborhood were similar to me. Our parents had similar types of jobs, and we lived in similar houses. However, at my school, I met children from richer and poorer families. Some children lived in apartments or on farms. I learned to get along with many different kinds of children, so I can get along with many kinds of people today. Because private schools in my country cost a lot of money, only rich children can go there. Therefore, children at private schools don't interact with poorer children. However, it is important to learn to interact with all kinds of people, for you will meet them at some point in your life.

Your turn *page 38*

Students can also exchange essays with a partner. However, be sensitive to cases where weaker students may feel criticized by stronger students.

B Write the final draft *page 38*

This is a good time to make sure that students understand any special requirements you have for essay format, such as what information should go on the first page, whether they are to use a pencil, pen, or computer, and so on. Make sure students know when the final draft is due.

V   FOLLOWING UP

A Share your writing *page 39*

Sharing writing with others is a valuable activity. It emphasizes writing as communication, develops community, and provides closure. This activity should take place before the final draft is turned in, so that the sharing will take place before you have marked and graded the essays. Remind students that at this point, they are only making positive comments about the essays they hear.

B Check your progress *page 39*

The *Progress Check* is the final step in each chapter. It is essential for students to evaluate their progress as they complete each essay. For this first time, however, you may want to provide some help. One way to do this is to photocopy page 39 and have students turn it in (uncompleted) with their essays. Then you can fill in the *Progress Check* for each student. Another way is for you to have a brief conference with each student to discuss the *Progress Check* and how it can be filled in. One additional way is for you to give students time in class to look over the returned essays, to determine their strengths and weaknesses based on your comments, and then to fill out their own *Progress Checks*. If you choose the third way, you can circulate around the room during the activity, checking the students' responses and providing assistance. The value of having students fill out the form in the book is that they won't misplace it, and it will be easier for them to refer to it throughout the course.

Problem-Solution Essays

For Chapter 2, students will look at some statistics and read a student essay about how sleep affects school performance. The chapter inspires students to identify a problem that is worth writing about and to brainstorm some possible solutions. Students will learn to organize an essay around the solution(s) they are proposing. They will study how to write an introduction, thesis, and conclusion, specifically for a problem-solution essay. They will learn to include their readers in their essay. They will learn ways to avoid making overgeneralizations, especially by using modals in conditional sentences.

With your students, read the chapter introduction on page 41. Ask, *What problems have you read or heard about lately in the news? What problems have you dealt with in school?* Prompt students as needed to elicit answers.

I GETTING STARTED

A Think about the sample essay topic *page 42*

To open the topic of sleep and school performance, ask students how much sleep they got last night. Write their numbers on the board. As a class, discuss how much sleep is enough. Again, write students' opinions on the board. Then look at the bar graph on page 42. As a class or in small groups, have students discuss the questions at the bottom of the page.

Answers

1 70 percent of such students will have trouble waking up in the morning; 64 percent will feel tired during class; 48 percent will daydream in class; and 15 percent will fall asleep in class.
2–5 Answers will vary.

B Read the sample essay *pages 43–44*

Read or have a student read aloud the focus question before the class reads the essay. After students have read the essay, put them in pairs to discuss the problem and the solution discussed in the essay. After the discussion, get an overview of students' responses to the two focus questions, *Has the writer convinced you that the problem is serious?* and *Is the solution reasonable?* Encourage students to explain their answers.

If you wish, students can discuss these additional questions in small groups or as a class. Write the questions on the board.

1 In addition to lack of sleep, what else might cause you to daydream in class?
2 In addition to lack of sleep, what else might cause you to feel tired?
3 When you don't get enough sleep, what is usually the reason?

Notice the essay structure *page 44*

Read through the information box, *Problem-Solution Essays*, with your students. This box introduces the main content of a problem-solution essay.

Practice 1 *page 44*

Have students answer these questions individually according to their understanding of the student essay. Then have them compare answers with a partner or in a small group. As students discuss their answers, encourage them to share ideas, rather than simply to figure out who is "right" and who is "wrong." Instruct students to refer specifically to the contents of the essay in order to explain their thinking. The task guides students to discover the essay's purpose, structure, and key features. Since these elements are important for students' own writing, go over answers with the whole class.

Possible answers

1 a
2 The problem is that sleepy students bother others.
3 Thesis statement: To solve these problems, I think that teachers should make sleep a part of the class requirement.
  It proposes making sleep a part of the class requirement.
4 Yes, the explanation helps me to understand how sleep would be recorded, tracked, and graded.
5 b
6 Yes, the writer convinces me by pointing out how rules about language and dress put forth a higher standard in those areas.
7 Conclusion: Teachers should motivate students to get enough sleep by making a sleep requirement and by making sure that students obey it. Body: Teachers can also use other grading policies to strengthen the sleep requirement. Conclusion: This is no different from many other types of rules that students routinely follow in order to get a high level of academic performance. Body: The sleep requirement should be like any other activity that students are graded on, such as homework, attendance, tests, or participation. Conclusion: If teachers show that they value rested students, it is probable that students will value their rest more, too. Body: If a school sets high expectations about behavior, students will be more likely to work to reach those expectations.
8 This solution might help to solve the problem, because students care about their grades. However, it wouldn't completely solve it, because students are busy and some of them like to go to bed late.

D Select a topic *page 45*

Read through the information box, *Choosing a Topic*, with your students. Talk about why it is important for students to think of a problem they or somebody they know has had. List the reasons on the board. (Examples: Their experience gives them some knowledge. Their experience gives them some passion about the topic. They will likely already have ideas about how to solve the problem. It is easier to write about something specific than something hypothetical or not of personal concern.)

Practice 2 *page 45*

Model the process of filling out this chart for the first possible essay topic, "Some students bully other students at school." As you answer the question in each column, ask yourself *Why? (Is the problem relevant to you? Why?)* Answer each *why* question in order to model how you would think through each question. Give students about 10–15 minutes to complete this chart. Then go over their answers, discussing their thoughts and reasons.

Answers will vary.

Your turn *page 46*

Make sure every student chooses or writes a topic. Point out that students may be able to slightly reword these topics to make them more interesting for themselves. For example, discuss how item 3 could be changed to read: *Nervous people can find it difficult to meet or socialize with others,* or *Shy people can find it difficult to find a job.*

E Brainstorm *page 46*

Read through the information box, *Freewriting*, with your students. If students are unfamiliar with freewriting, model your own freewriting on the chalkboard. For example, you could freewrite about the topic of learning vocabulary or speaking in front of a class. In order to be effective, your model should include abbreviated words, lists, random grammar, and so on. Freewriting is best done with a time limit, as it focuses and pushes students. Time your modeling for two minutes. Make sure to include solutions.

Practice 3 *pages 46–47*

As they read this freewriting, remind students to focus on possible solutions. The problem, naturally, is mentioned several times throughout this freewriting. However, more than the problem, the potential solutions are important, as these will be the basis for the organization of the essay.

Answers

Children in America are getting really fat. It's a shameful problem. Some people in the world are starving, and Americans are eating too much. Many reasons for their weight problems. First, they eat too much. <u>They should eat less.</u> At restaurants in America, they serve huge portions. Nobody can finish it. <u>Need smaller portions, eat until full.</u> What is the prize for eating a big meal? Dessert. Dessert, sweets, candy, cookies. <u>Should eat less sugar!</u>

Candy is a prize in a lot of situations. Ex: Some schools give candy as a prize for doing homework or winning a competition. <u>Food shouldn't be a prize.</u> Another big problem is snacking. Kids always snack . . . home, school, camp. Too many snacks! American kids snack all of the time — libraries, bus stops, parking lots, cars, movies, watching TV. Bad eating habits. <u>Need meals, not snacks.</u> When they get older, they will continue with these bad habits. <u>Start good eating habits young.</u> <u>Should sit down and eat healthy meals.</u> Americans eat while they walk down the street. In my country, this is socially unacceptable. Eating is one problem, but no exercise is the next reason. Kids sit around too much. Watch TV. Drive everywhere. No walking or biking. When we visit my parents' country, everybody <u>is walking or biking.</u> In America, most of my friends have video game systems, computers, and TVs in their bedroom. Even keep snacks in their bedroom! Schools don't help. Gym class is only once or twice a week. <u>Need more sports!</u>

Your turn *page 47*

Time students as they brainstorm for five minutes. Encourage students to do their freewriting in their notebook or on paper that they can keep. Discourage freewriting on scratch paper, as students will repeatedly refer back to their freewriting for ideas as they produce their essays. After students freewrite, have them check to make sure that they have included one or two solutions.

F Discuss your ideas with others *page 47*

Encourage students to use this opportunity to explore new ideas, new ways of thinking about the problem, and new solutions. Remind students that their freewriting is not a final product. While some ideas may end up in the final essay, others may not.

A Organize the essay *page 48*

Read through the information box, *The Structure of a Problem-Solution Essay*, with your students. Think of a problem that immediately affects your class of students, however small. For example, there is never enough chalk, or the room gets too hot in the afternoon. As a class, brainstorm several possible solutions to the problem. Then write on the board two outlines for two different possible problem-solution essays.

- **Type 1: Several solutions**

  Introduction   Room is hot in afternoon: many ways to solve
  Paragraph   Close blinds before sun reaches room
  Paragraph   Open windows during class
  Paragraph   Get a fan

- **Type 2: One solution**

  Introduction   Room is hot in afternoon: one way to solve
  Paragraph   Get a different room: east side of building is cooler at that time
  Paragraph   No need to mess with curtains, blinds, windows, fans, etc.

Practice 4 *pages 48–49*

You may want to help students get started by reading through the two outlines together. Then, rather than telling them the correct answers, point out the information in the outlines that will help them to find the answers.

Answers

1 a
2 a – IV (third body paragraph)
  b – II (first body paragraph)
  c – III (second body paragraph)

Your turn *page 49*

Have students look again at their freewriting and at their notes from their group discussions about their freewriting to decide whether their essays will focus on one or several solutions. Remind students that their essays do not need to include every solution that was named in their freewriting. For example, if a student has one main solution, and a small, optional side solution, the student may want the essay to focus only on the main solution, leading to a Type 2 essay.

B Plan the introduction *page 50*

Read through the information box, *Introduction to a Problem-Solution Essay*, with your students. Explain to students that the introductory paragraph is usually the only paragraph in a problem-solution essay that focuses primarily on the problem, and it does this only to lead to the thesis statement. Explain that if an entire problem-solution essay focused primarily on the problem, then it could be seen as a "complaint essay." This would be a non-standard essay and is not being taught in this chapter.

As a class, refer to the sample essay, "Eight Hours a Night," on pages 43–44. Together, reread the introduction. Discuss these topics:

Is there a hook?
What is the problem?
When and where is it a problem?
Who and what causes the problem?
Who is affected by the problem?
What is the solution?

Practice 5 *page 50*

Give students time to examine the introductory paragraph. Encourage students to mark it up by underlining or highlighting. This will help them to focus on the key material in the paragraph. Ask each pair or group to answer one question.

Answers

1 " . . . they may not want you."
2 The local shopping mall is considering kicking out its teenage shoppers.
3 It's a problem in the mall, especially on weekend evenings.
4 Teenagers cause the problem.
5 "Other mall-goers" are affected.
6 The solution is to bring teen patrols into the malls on weekend evenings.

Your turn *page 50*

As students plan their introductory paragraphs, remind them that they are just planning its contents now. Later, when they actually draft the paragraph, they will pick and choose from the ideas they now generate. Later still, when they write, they will decide on wording and the organization of their ideas.

C Compose the thesis statement *page 51*

Read through the information box, *Offering a Solution*, with your students. Once again, help students to focus on the fact that the thesis statement for a problem-solution essay focuses on the *solution*, not the problem. When people think about problems, they often feel passionate and frustrated, and this can cause them to focus on the problem. However, such a focus is not the thrust of a problem-solution essay.

Practice 6 *page 51*

Answer

3 In order to maintain a healthy weight, American children need to change many lifestyle habits related to when they eat, how much they eat, and how much physical activity they get. This thesis is the only one that covers the three main solutions mentioned in the freewriting.

Your turn *page 51*

Students can write the paragraph in class or as homework.

D Make an outline *page 51*

Read through the information box, *Outlining*, with your students. Emphasize that the outlining process gives students another chance to generate and consider new ideas.

Practice 7 *page 52*

Answers

1 The third paragraph is not included in the essay.
2 The writer decided to keep point B, that students would lose points, and she put it instead into the second paragraph of the essay.
3 The writer softened point B, which says that students follow rules. Instead, her essay says that when schools set high expectations, students are more likely to reach them.

Your turn *page 53*

As students begin work on their outlines, remind them that outlining is often a messy process. Outlines often include lots of crossed-out words, arrows, question marks, and so on. A draft of an outline would rarely look as neat as the outline for "Eight Hours a Night." Encourage students first to draft an outline, and later to write it out neatly.

E Plan the conclusion *page 53*

Read through the information box, *The Conclusion*, with your students. In a problem-solution essay, the conclusion often repeats essentially the same information as the introductory paragraph. As with other parts of the essay, its ultimate focus must remain on the solution, not the problem.

Practice 8 *pages 53–54*

After students have answered the question, discuss their responses.

Possible answers

1 Not a good closing sentence: too general
2 May be okay, comments optimistically about the likely success of the solution
3 Not a good closing sentence: doesn't relate to the solution
4 Good closing sentence: optimistic, focuses on readers and others

Your turn *page 54*

Students can write this in class or as homework.

F Discuss your ideas with others *page 54*

As a class, read through the questions. Encourage students to focus their discussion on these specific questions. Remind them that they will likely find wording and grammar issues that may seem wrong, but at this point, such issues are not the focus of the discussion.

G Write the first draft *page 54*

Writing the first draft is likely to be a time-consuming step, despite the thorough groundwork students have already done. This is an excellent homework step, though it can also be done in class. Facilities permitting, it makes good sense for students to write the first draft on a computer. Remind them to print the draft for use in class, labeled "first draft."

III REVISING YOUR WRITING

A Benefit from peer feedback *page 55*

Circulate around the room during this activity and make sure students only check for what is on the checklist. Make sure students have adequate time (at least 20 minutes) to read and review their partner's essay, and also sufficient time to meet with each other to go over the feedback forms (about 10 minutes).

B Include your reader *page 56*

Read through the information box, *Including Your Reader*, with your students. The box names four common techniques for involving readers, with examples for each. As a class, try to generate an additional example of each of the four techniques. Then, as a class, try to think of one or two additional ways that a writer can include his or her reader.

Practice 9 *page 57*

Possible answers

1 Introduction B includes the reader more.
2 The writer starts with a question for the reader, uses the second person (if you, you may), and describes how the problem relates to a large group of people (most people, many people).
3 The writer could write not only about herself, but also about others. Also, the writer could explain how the problem relates to others. The writer could ask questions. The writer could mention the emotions, hopes, and fears of the reader.

Your turn *page 57*

Remind students that in order to judge their essays, they must look specifically, word-by-word, at what they've written. They must consider each statement as it will affect the reader. In other words, scanning their writing for its overall gist is insufficient.

C Think critically *page 58*

Read through the information box, *Evaluating Solutions*, with your students. Discuss the sample sentences about the correlation between smoke and cancer. Point out to students that it is difficult to prove a causal relationship. Remind students that just because something has happened once does not mean that it will always happen that way. Just because a student has had a given experience with some problem does not mean that every person with the same problem would have the same experience.

Practice 10 *pages 58–59*

After students have completed these questions, discuss their answers.

Answers

1 Inaccurate. If you get good grades in school, you are more likely to get a good job.
2 OK
3 Inaccurate. Driving more slowly can lead to fewer road accidents.
4 Inaccurate. If students don't play video games, they may have more opportunities to make friends.
5 Inaccurate. Cutting up your credit cards can help keep you out of debt.
6 Inaccurate. Rested students may have a better chance of getting higher grades.
7 Inaccurate. Many boys on sports teams are popular.
8 Inaccurate. Smoking may cause cancer.
9 OK

Your turn *page 59*

Circulate around the class, sitting with individual students to look at their essays. Try to find at least one sentence per essay that could benefit from more critical thought. In offering this feedback to the student, ask the student a question about his or her idea. Rather than telling the student the problem with the sentence, asking a question can inspire the student to identify the problem.

D Make revision decisions *page 59*

Remind the class that each student must make his or her own decision about using the suggestions given during the peer feedback.

E Write the second draft *page 59*

Students can write their second drafts in class or as homework. Make sure that the second draft includes the label "second draft."

IV EDITING YOUR WRITING

A Use hedging to avoid overgeneralization *page 60*

Read through the information box, *Hedging*, with your students. Review the prior information box and exercise on critical thinking (pages 58–59). To teach the idea of overgeneralization and to show the benefits of hedging, have students work in pairs to create sentences with broad generalizations. Have them put their sentences on the board. As a class, talk about the sentences and work to soften their claims. Start with your own example, such as *All ESL teachers have experience living overseas.*

Practice 11 *page 61*

> In my classes, sleep-deprived students (tend to) disturb other students, and this (can) make it hard to learn. No matter what class they are in, sleep-deprived students (are likely to) cause problems. For example, they (rarely) contribute to the classroom topic. If they do say anything in the class, it's (usually) just to ask a question that was already answered. Such sleepy students (can) even kill motivation for students who are awake. When I see five people sleeping with their heads on top of their desks, (it is possible that) I will feel sleepy too, especially if it is a boring or an early morning class. Another problem with (many) students who don't get enough sleep is that (it is not unusual) for them to arrive late to class, interrupting whatever is happening. To solve these problems, (I think) that teachers should make sleep a part of the class requirement.

Practice 12 *page 61*

You may want to have volunteers write answers on the board so that you can discuss errors and talk about alternative wording.

Possible answers

2 After giving birth, a large number of women may face challenges in controlling their weight.
3 Many students who carry heavy backpacks are likely to experience back trouble.
4 Quite a few people in my company frequently work overtime.
5 Most of my classmates say that they tend to listen to music while doing their homework.
6 It is possible that some climbers at those altitudes will run out of breath and need to breathe from an oxygen tank.
7 Many experts believe that diet soda is probably just as bad for your heath as regular soda.
8 It seems that shy students rarely contribute to class discussions.

Practice 13 *page 62*

Possible answers

1 Eating a large breakfast can improve students' performance during the day.
2 Drinking more than three cups of coffee a day is probably bad for your health.
3 Most students who can't get parking permits on campus should take the bus.
4 Putting at least five copies of each course book on reserve in the library is likely to help students save money on textbooks.
5 Many students complain about the complicated course registration process.

Your turn *page 62*

As students check their drafts, circulate around the class, looking at students' papers. If you see a word in an essay that could be softened, point to it or circle it in the student's paper.

B Use conditionals to hedge *page 62*

Read through the information box, *Using Conditionals to Hedge*, with your students. Students at this level have often studied the basic conditional, "If X, then Y." Point out that this form is rarely taught with the option of using modals. As a class, you should be able to generate a variety of conditional sentences, rewriting them with various modals to weaken the degree of certainty.

Practice 14 *page 63*

Answers

1 If those students turn in identical essays, the teacher *may want* to talk to them after class.
2 Students *might be* late to the assembly if the bus arrives late to school.
3 If you can't commit to team practice on Thursdays, you *may not be* able to compete in all of the games.
4 If Anna forgets her password again, the bank *could* simply refuse to give her another ATM card.
5 You *may* get a better grade if you do the extra credit assignments.
6 If you don't eat breakfast, you *may* feel tired in the afternoon.

Practice 15 *page 63*

Possible answers

2 If you recycle all your glass and plastic containers, you could save money on your garbage bill.
3 If you buy your computer online, you might have to pay a shipping cost.
4 If you review new vocabulary regularly, even when you don't have a test, you will remember more words.
5 If you carry an extra sweater in your backpack, you may be happy to have it.
6 If you read one book a month, you may improve your writing.

Practice 16 *page 63*

Possible answers

The second and third sentences contain hedging. The first does not. The sentence without hedging is trying to make its point optimistically.

2 If a school sets high expectations about behavior, students <u>will be more likely</u> to work to reach those expectations.
3 If teachers show that they value rested students, <u>it is probable</u> that students will value their rest more, too.

C Punctuate conditionals *page 64*

Read through the information box, *Punctuating Conditionals*, with your students. Put more samples of conditionals on the board, or have students generate their own samples as the basis for more class practice with conditionals.

Practice 17 *page 64*

Answers

> Second, if high school students ~~will~~ learn more about U.S. history, they will likely be more active citizens when they are older. If they understand the events and trials that have led to universal suffrage, students *will* value their right to vote. If they appreciate the historical development of voting rights in the United States, it is possible that they will even feel honored by their right to vote. They will surely go to the polls and cast their vote. Voting is just the beginning of their participation as citizens, and it's an important step, because it makes them feel a part of the political process. If they ~~will~~ feel that they are members of this process, many of them will surely be inspired to participate even more. They will want to follow issues and get to know candidates if they realize that they are part of the decision-making process.

Your turn *page 64*

Have students check and mark their second drafts.

D Write the final draft *page 64*

When students turn in their final drafts, you may also want to collect their first and second drafts again as well. This can help you to comment on the changes and improvements across drafts.

V FOLLOWING UP

A Share your writing *page 65*

Read through the information box, *Small-Group Read-Aloud*, with your students. After all the group members' essays have been read, choose the one essay that you think could be shared with a broader audience. With the class, discuss who that audience is. A problem-solution essay might logically be shared with the person or group responsible for or affected by the problem. For example, an essay about long cafeteria lines at school might be shared with the person who runs the cafeteria. If appropriate, encourage the students to share the chosen essay with a broader audience.

B Check your progress *page 65*

When completing this progress check, students will have the benefit of your feedback. However, encourage students to consider not only your input, but also their own feelings about their writing. The progress check should reflect their current understanding of their writing.

Chapter 2

Comparison-Contrast Essays

3

For Chapter 3, students will consider different aspects of a similar issue and then write an essay highlighting their similarities and/or differences. Students will organize their ideas by using a Venn diagram and will write a sentence supporting the thesis statement that shows the scope of the essay by listing its main points. They will also learn and practice specific language to emphasize similarities and differences, evaluate their ideas and sentences for relevancy, and use language appropriate for an academic context.

With your students, read the chapter introduction on page 67. Ask, *What are some reasons people compare products or ideas? What have you compared recently?* Elicit answers from volunteers.

I GETTING STARTED

A Think about the sample essay topic *page 68*

Go over the chart briefly with the whole class to make sure students understand all of the vocabulary and what the chart shows (how many million adult Americans did these activities on a typical day in 2004). Then have students answer the questions in small groups. If possible, mix groups by age, gender, and nationality. If you like, ask one student in each group to take notes and to be responsible for sharing some of the group's answers with the whole class.

Answers

1 Most popular: use e-mail. Least popular: participate in an online auction.
2 People go online more for social reasons (assuming that e-mail is social and not work-related – students can disagree about this).
3–7 Answers will vary.

B Read the sample essay *pages 69–70*

Read or have a student read aloud the focus question before students read the essay. Ask students to think about the question, as well as the author's purpose for writing the essay, as they read. After they finish reading, have them briefly answer the focus questions with a partner. As a class, discuss their answers.

If you wish, students can discuss these additional questions in small groups or as a class. Write the questions on the board.

1 Do you communicate differently online? If so, how?
2 Have you ever played an online game? If so, which one(s)?

C Notice the essay structure *page 70*

Read through the information box, *Comparison-Contrast Essays*, with your students. Make sure students understand that typically writers compare seemingly different things and contrast seemingly similar things. Point out that there probably isn't a strong reason to describe the differences between things that are obviously different (for example, between an SUV and a bicycle), or the similarities between things that are clearly similar (for example, a laptop and a desktop computer). In addition, the purpose for comparing or contrasting should be clear from the start.

Practice 1 *page 71*

Have students work through Practice 1 with a partner, or first answer the questions individually and then compare answers with classmates.

Answers

1 Thesis statement: In fact, online friends have several advantages over face-to-face friends.
2 Topic sentences:
   First body paragraph: The Internet offers special methods of communication.
   Second body paragraph: The feelings you have communicating online are special, too.
   Third body paragraph: The most important advantage of online friends for me is the possibility of finding friends without any geographical restriction.
3 Mostly contrasting.
4–7 Answers will vary.
8 He encourages readers to consider making some online friends.

D Select a topic *page 71*

Read through the information box, *Topics*, with your students. To get them thinking about potential topics, ask them to remember a decision they recently made (or will soon make) by comparing or contrasting, such as which computer to buy, where to go on vacation, or what subject to study in college. Use one example to discuss whether students would compare or contrast.

Practice 2 *pages 71–72*

After you check answers, ask students to notice how their choice to compare or contrast depends on their purpose for writing.

Answers

1	a	4	a
2	b	5	a
3	b	6	b

Your turn *page 72*

Circulate while students are working to check their topics and offer help if necessary.

E Brainstorm *page 73*

Read through the information box, *Venn Diagrams*, with your students. If any students find it awkward to write their ideas in circles, they can instead use three columns, with one column on the left for the first topic, one column on the right for the second topic, and a middle column for ideas about both topics.

Practice 3 *pages 73–74*

Students can copy and fill in the Venn diagrams on a separate sheet of paper, if they need more space.

Answers

Topic: online friends versus face-to-face friends
Purpose: to recommend making online friends

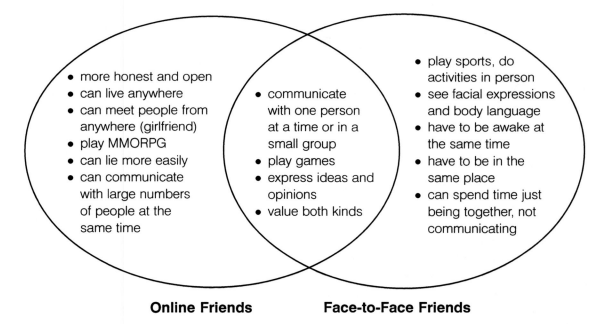

Online Friends   **Face-to-Face Friends**

Practice 4 *page 74*

Answers

The writer didn't use *see facial expressions and body language* or *can lie more easily* because they aren't advantages of online friends. The writer also didn't include *have to be awake at the same time*, a disadvantage of communicating with friends face-to-face.

Your turn *page 74*

Students should brainstorm by themselves. They can do this in class or for homework. Remind students that they will keep and refer to their Venn diagrams throughout this chapter as they write their essays.

F Discuss your ideas with others *page 74*

Make sure students have pencils with them when they discuss their ideas, so they can add more information to their diagrams if appropriate.

▊ PREPARING THE FIRST DRAFT

A Compose the thesis statement *page 75*

Remind students to look back at their brainstormed ideas as they write their thesis statements. The thesis statement should express the purpose for writing the essay; that is, it should indicate why they are comparing or contrasting their subjects. If possible, check and approve each student's thesis statement before continuing to the next activity.

B Edit your brainstorming *page 75*

Remind students that they should ask themselves whether each idea in their brainstorming relates to the thesis statement. They can either cross out ideas in their diagrams that do not support their thesis statement, or, if they find themselves crossing out too many ideas or ideas that they want to keep, they can reevaluate and change their thesis statements. You may want to quickly check each student's diagram to see that edits have been made.

C Add a sentence that shows scope *page 75*

Read through the information box, *Showing the Scope of the Essay*, with your students. Explain that since clarity is a major goal of academic essays in English, a sentence that shows scope strengthens an essay by letting the reader know the writer's main points in advance. In academic English, there are rarely any "surprise endings," and a reader should know the main ideas as soon as possible. A phrase showing the scope can be part of the thesis statement, rather than a separate sentence that comes before or after. However, this can also make a thesis statement too long or complex, so sometimes it is preferable to divide the information into two sentences.

Practice 5 *page 76*

After you check the answers to Practice 5, as an extension, you can ask students to identify the part of the thesis statement in the introduction to the sample essay (*Essay Writing Basics*, page 4) that shows scope: *adolescents, businesspeople, and others who can't control their spending.*

Answers

> Chapter 1: *It was very difficult for me at first, but eventually I learned how to make true friends, obey rules, and return my parents' love.* This comes before the thesis statement.
> Chapter 2: There is no sentence previewing the scope.

Your turn *page 76*

Although it is not necessary to have a sentence showing scope in every academic essay, tell students that it is an important skill to practice, so such a sentence is required in their essay assignment in this chapter.

D Organize your essay *page 76*

Read through the information box, *Organizing a Comparison-Contrast Essay*, with your students. Point out that block style will work more easily if students are not discussing the same number of aspects of A and B, and that alternating style will be more successful if students are comparing or contrasting the same aspects of A and B.

Practice 6 *pages 76–77*

Answers

> Paragraph 1: Alternating style
> Paragraph 2: Block style

Practice 7 *pages 77–78*

Go over the example on page 78 with the whole class to make sure that students understand what to do.

After you go over the answers, point out to students that the block style is not completely rigid; the topic sentence will still be about B. If you wish, you can analyze the other body paragraphs, too. Students will notice that the topic sentence is always from B, and in the case of the third body paragraph, there is a concluding sentence from B as well. Point out that in most actual writing, a style is mostly block or mostly alternating, but need not be rigidly one or the other.

> ᴮThe feelings you have communicating online are special, too. | ᴬWhen I am talking in person with a friend, I am more hesitant and shyer. ᴬI keep some of my ideas hidden. | ᴮIn <u>contrast</u>, when I am writing e-mails or IMing (instant messaging), I am more honest and open. ᴮOnline communication feels safer and more confidential to me, and I don't fear people judging or criticizing me. ᴮI express my opinions more directly, and I share thoughts that I would never say out loud. ᴮI can't explain why this happens, but my friends tell me they feel the same way. ᴮI know when I receive e-mails and IMs, even from people I have never seen, they share more personal information than my face-to-face friends do. ᴮThis kind of open and honest expression is a relief to me.
>
> Organization: block

Your turn page 78

After students have thought about the organization for their essays, have them write down the type of organization they will use in their brainstorming notes.

E Make an outline page 78

Remind students that the more detailed their outline is, the easier it will be for them to write the first draft. The outline can be done in class or assigned as homework.

Practice 8 page 78

While students are discussing their outlines, circulate to answer questions and check their progress.

Answers will vary.

F Use language for comparing and contrasting page 79

Read through the information box, *Language for Comparing and Contrasting*, with your students. Explain that these phrases greatly help the reader in following the writer's logic. If your students need review with these structures, elicit examples from volunteers and write them on the board.

Practice 9 page 79

After you go over the answers, point out to students that in paragraphs 2, 3, and 4, the phrases they underlined show the reader where the writer is switching from idea A to B.

Answers

In paragraph 2: On the other hand
In paragraph 3: In contrast
In paragraph 4: on the other hand
In paragraph 5: both; unlike

Practice 10 pages 79–80

Answers

1 Unlike	4 On the other hand	7 Neither; nor
2 On the other hand	5 While	8 Like
3 Both; and	6 Unlike	9 In contrast

Practice 11 *page 80*

Point out to students that they do not need to combine the sentences but rather to connect them using a transition word or phrase. In some cases, two sentences will be combined into one sentence, but in other cases, not.

Possible answers

1 If you live at home while you attend college, you don't have to worry about housework and cooking. On the other hand, if you live by yourself in an apartment, you will have to take care of your home as well as your homework.
2 Online friends don't know everything about you. Similarly, face-to-face friends only know the information you choose to share with them.
3 When you read a book, you move from one page sequentially to the next page. In contrast, when you read online, you can move from one page to many different pages just by clicking on different links.
4 When you write with pen and paper, you can easily cross out ideas you don't like and add new ideas. Similarly, when you use a computer, you can delete ideas you don't want to use and type new information.

Your turn *page 80*

Students can write in class or as homework. Remind them to check their thesis statement and Venn diagram before they write and to follow their outline.

G Write the first draft *page 80*

Remind students that it may be easiest to write their introduction, hook, or title last.

▊ REVISING YOUR WRITING

A Benefit from peer feedback *page 81*

Circulate around the room during this activity and make sure that students' responses are complete and clear. Make sure students have adequate time to read and review their partners' essays and also sufficient time to meet with each other to go over the feedback forms.

B Connecting paragraphs *page 82*

Read through the information box, *Connecting Paragraphs to the Introduction*, with your students. Explain that the topic sentences of the body paragraphs will express the same ideas as were previewed in the scope sentence, but will not be worded exactly the same way. For another example of this, have them check the scope sentence and topic sentences in the sample essay in Chapter 1 on page 15.

Practice 12 *page 82*

Possible answers

. . . American and British English have <u>different spellings</u>, <u>different grammar</u>, and <u>different idioms</u>.

1 Some common differences in spelling show that American and British English are not exactly the same.
2 Both American and British English have many similarities, but there are still some important differences in grammar.
3 While Americans and British citizens can usually understand each other, sometimes different idioms lead to confusion.

Your turn *page 82*

Remind students that they can (and in fact should) vary the wording of their topic sentences slightly so that they are not copied directly from the sentence showing scope. Circulate while students are working to help out with this, if necessary.

C Critical thinking *page 83*

Read through the information box, *Keeping Ideas Relevant*, with your students. Remind students that it is fine to include all ideas in their brainstorming, but that in the final draft, only ideas that explain and support the thesis statement belong in the essay. One time to edit out irrelevant ideas is after brainstorming but before writing the first draft. However, it's a good idea to check again after the first draft has been written.

Practice 13 *page 83*

Students can discuss which sentences are irrelevant and why with a partner or a small group, or you can discuss the answers together as a whole class. Encourage students to articulate why the irrelevant sentence does not support the topic sentence.

Answers

(irrelevant sentences)
Paragraph 1: You might need to buy a carrying case, though. / These days, it's easy to find Internet cafes in every city, so that's also very convenient.
Paragraph 2: It took me a long time to get used to the British accents. / I never did anything like that again, though.
Paragraph 3: However, I don't like it when I get on a plane and the movie is something I've just seen recently. / Then I prefer to read a book.

D Make revision decisions *page 83*

Remind the class that each student must make his or her own decisions about using the suggestions given during peer feedback.

E **Write the second draft** *page 83*

Students can write the second draft in class or as homework.

IV EDITING YOUR WRITING

A **Use academic language** *page 84*

Read through the information box, *Academic Language*, with your students. Explain that casual English is not "bad," and is of course more appropriate than academic English in other contexts. If you have students who share a common native language, ask them to think of some examples in their own language of casual and formal language. One problem for nonnative English speakers, of course, is that they don't always know whether a vocabulary word is casual or formal. The only way to learn is through experience. If they make mistakes with overly casual vocabulary, a good peer reviewer or a teacher can point it out and suggest more formal words.

Practice 14 *page 84*

Possible answers

> Most students of English know some of the common differences in ~~vocab~~ *vocabulary* between American and British English. Americans ride an elevator, but ~~Brits~~ *British people* use a lift. Americans live in an apartment, while British people live in a flat. However, those differences aren't ~~really a big deal~~ *important*. Ninety-six percent of the vocabulary in American and British English is the same, so there are ~~way~~ *significantly* ~~more~~ *more* similarities than differences. ~~What's more~~ *Furthermore,* because of ~~TV~~ *television,* books, movies, ~~etc.~~ *and so on,* most people already know the common differences. Even if they read an unfamiliar word, ~~I bet~~ *they can* guess its meaning from the context. Students should think of the differences as ~~cool~~ *interesting* and not ~~get stressed out~~ *be bothered* by them.

Your turn *page 84*

Circulate while students are working to help out with vocabulary choices if necessary. When students have finished, ask volunteers to tell which informal words they changed in their essays.

B **Use comparative structures** *page 85*

Read through the information box, *Comparing Adjectives and Adverbs*, with your students. You may wish to have students cover the rules and examples in the book and ask them if they already know the rules. Write them on the board as students explain them. Remind students to use adjectives when they are comparing nouns, and adverbs when they are comparing verbs.

Practice 15 *page 85*

Read through the information box, *Intensifying Comparisons*, with your students. While they are probably already familiar with the meaning of these words, they may not be using them regularly in their writing. Ask volunteers to make up sentences using some of the intensifiers. Then have students complete Practice 15.

You may wish to also ask students to indicate whether the words they found were adjectives or adverbs.

Answers

Students should circle the following comparative adjectives and adverbs.
First paragraph: *more deeply; (more) honestly.*
Third paragraph: *more hesitant; shyer; more honest; (more) open; safer; more confidential; more directly.* Some students may also find *share more personal information.*
Fourth paragraph: *most important; more honestly; (more) openly, more quickly; (more) easily.*

Practice 16 *page 86*

Answers

>   Business class is ~~more~~ *more* significantly comfortable ~~as~~ *than* economy class. First of all, the seats are ~~more wide~~ *wider* and ~~more soft~~ *softer*. I can stretch out my legs ~~easier~~ *more easily* because of the extra space. A second advantage is that the food is far more delicious. The meals are ~~more fresh~~ *fresher* in business class than in economy class, and they're prepared better, too. The movies that are shown in business class are more ~~recently~~ *recent* and more popular. Even the flight attendants are somewhat friendlier to customers in business class. They speak ~~politer~~ *more politely* and give ~~good~~ *better* service. Even if it ~~considerably~~ *considerably* costs more money, I will always fly business class.

Your turn *page 86*

Students can check their essays in class or as homework. If they are comfortable doing so, they can exchange with a partner and check one another's essays.

C Write the final draft *page 86*

Make sure students know when their final drafts are due. Ask them to turn in the first draft with the final draft so that you can see their progress. You may also ask them to attach their brainstorming notes.

V FOLLOWING UP

A Share your writing *page 86*

As far as possible, have students work in groups with others who wrote on different topics, so that they will be able to discuss a wide range and variety of ideas.

B Check your progress *page 87*

Students can complete the *Progress Check* in class or as homework. You could even ask students to e-mail their *Progress Checks* to you. Students can look back at their *Progress Checks* from Chapter 1 as well as Chapter 2 to note improvements as they go through the chapters.

Chapter 4 — Persuasive Essays

For Chapter 4, students will read a sample essay that persuades readers to consider ways to change Japanese society so that women will be inspired to have more children. The chapter encourages students to think of arguments that support their position, and to consider a reader's possible counterarguments. Students will learn how to organize a persuasive essay, using language to present arguments and counterarguments. Students will practice writing a catchy hook. They will study various types of support that can strengthen their essays.

With your students, read the chapter introduction on page 89. As a class, talk about current, controversial topics in the news, in your town, or in your classroom.

I   GETTING STARTED

A   Think about the sample essay topic   *page 90*

Before reading the sample essay, students will look at statistics that show the declining birthrate in several countries around the world. To open the topic of declining birthrates, have students talk about births in their own families. Ask, for example: *How many children did your paternal grandparents have? How many did your maternal grandparents have? How many did your own parents have?* Record students' answers on the board. Based on your rough class survey, can the students see any trends?

Next, look at the bar graph on page 90. As a class or in small groups, have students discuss the questions at the bottom of the page.

B   Read the sample essay   *pages 91–92*

Read or have a student read aloud the focus question before students read the essay. Then have students read the sample essay, "Bringing Babies Back to Japan." After students read, put them in pairs to discuss the essay and the focus question. Have students been persuaded by the writer's position? If so, what were they persuaded of? If they were not persuaded, which points did they not accept?

If you wish, students can discuss these additional questions in small groups or as a class. Write the questions on the board.

1 In your opinion, who should be mostly responsible for raising children?
2 What are your attitudes about raising children?
3 Are your attitudes different from your parents' attitudes? Are your parents' attitudes different from *their* parents' attitudes?
4 What do you think has caused any changes of attitude?

C Notice the essay structure *page 92*

Read through the information box, *Organization of Persuasive Essays*, with your students. Point out that this information relates to a common organizational pattern for the paragraphs in persuasive essays. In this organization, the writer anticipates the reader's likely response to the essay's arguments, addressing it directly at the beginning of a paragraph.

Practice 1 *page 93*

As a class, discuss students' answers and ideas. Encourage students to think of other arguments in question 6.

Answers

1 Thesis statement: Japan's entire social structure, including families, businesses, and the government, must work together to encourage families to have babies.
2 Topic sentences: Paragraph 1: Now, Japanese women no longer seem interested solely in raising children, and society needs to accept this.
Paragraph 2: Japanese companies need to recognize their role in shaping families and think more about supporting them. (Also possible: Usually, people don't think of a company as a force in shaping families, but this attitude should be reconsidered.)
Paragraph 3: Even though the raising of children is not an easy job or a traditional job for Japanese men, we must accept that it is partly men's work, too.
Paragraph 4: It is the government's job to help make child raising more affordable.
3 Looking after children is hard work, and most Japanese men don't have experience with it. → Men must also participate in raising children.
Nobody wants to pay for another person's children. → Producing Japan's next generation is so important that the nation should offer attractive financial incentive for this work.
Many people consider child raising the work of women. → Women should be able to have a career and raise children.
It is not generally considered a company's job to help raise families. → Japanese companies need to make it easy for working parents to keep their jobs and have children, too.
4 In the fourth body paragraph, the counterargument comes later in the paragraph: *While it is true that many people don't want to pay higher taxes to support other people's children, producing the next generation of Japan is a question of our nation's existence.*

5 It summarizes the arguments, and it gives a final comment on the topic.

6 Answers will vary.

D Select a topic *page 94*

Read through the information box, *Choosing a Topic*, with your students. Ask a few students to share their topics with the class. Ask each student directly, *Do you like your topic? Are you excited to write about it?* A student who likes a topic is much more likely to write a good essay about it. Likewise, a student who doesn't like his or her topic should be encouraged to consider some alternatives. (Remember, however, that liking a topic alone is not sufficient basis for an essay.)

Practice 2 *page 94*

Answers

> My sister wants to have two kids. (4) She's an architect and she wants to keep her paid job. Child care is so expensive, they can't afford it. Lots of couples can't afford it. It makes me angry. (2) My sister is 37 and still has no children. This is sad because she really wants kids. Her husband can't help because of his company's rules. My friends and their families have the same problem. My pen pal in Norway says it's easier there. (3) They have great ideas. Companies offer affordable day care. Government gives tax incentives there. Men take leave to help raise children.
>
> Japanese culture doesn't train men to help with raising children. It's a huge problem. I know not everyone will agree with me, but everybody needs to work together to solve this problem. (1) Someday I want to have children, but I don't want to have to give up my career to do it. I'm not the only one. This affects everybody. (5)

Your turn *page 95*

Remind students that they are more likely to write effectively if they like their topic.

E Brainstorm arguments *page 95*

Give students five minutes to brainstorm arguments. Some students may already have specific arguments to support their point. They are free to write these down directly. However, they should still spend time brainstorming, as this may help them to develop their support, and it may help them to uncover other support for their topic.

F Discuss your ideas with others *page 95*

As they discuss their ideas with others, students should take notes. The purpose of the discussion is to generate ideas. Taking notes can help students, not only to remember what was said, but also to make and see new connections between ideas. This, in turn, can help them to envision the shape of their essay.

II PREPARING THE FIRST DRAFT

A Compose the thesis statement *page 96*

Read through the information box, *Persuasive Essay Thesis Statements*, with your students. Discuss why these four elements are considered essential in a thesis statement of a persuasive essay. As a class, look at the thesis statement in the sample essay and try to find its four main components. Some of the information overlaps, and this is normal, as the ideas are clearly intertwined.

Thesis statement: *Japan's entire social structure, including families, businesses, and the government, must work together to encourage families to have babies.*

Practice 3 *page 96*

Answers

1 a Effective because it clearly states the topic, the writer's opinion, a course of action, and its purpose.
   b Ineffective because it doesn't express writer's opinion or a course of action.
2 a Effective because it states the topic and the writer's opinion. It implies a course of action and its benefits.
   b Ineffective because it suggests no course of action.
3 a Ineffective because it states a fact rather than an opinion and offers no course of action.
   b Effective because it clearly states the topic, the writer's opinion, a course of action, and its purpose.
4 a Effective because it clearly states the topic and the writer's opinion. It implies a course of action and explains the reason.
   b Ineffective because it states a fact rather than an opinion and proposes no action.
5 a Effective because it clearly states the topic and the writer's opinion. It implies a course of action and explains the reason.
   b Ineffective because it states a fact rather than an opinion and proposes no action.
6 a Effective because it clearly states the topic, the writer's opinion, a course of action, and its purpose.
   b Ineffective because it doesn't propose a course of action.

Your turn *page 96*

Remind students that the first drafts of the thesis statements will not likely be the last. A good thesis statement often requires several rewrites.

B Plan the introduction *page 97*

Read through the information box, *Catchy Hooks*, with your students. Then ask one student to share his or her thesis with the class. As a class, brainstorm some possible hooks to match the thesis. Write all ideas on the board.

Your turn *page 97*

Remind students that this exercise is just meant to generate some options and discuss them with a partner. They do not have to settle on a hook right now. Indeed, they may find that new ideas come to them later.

C Organize your arguments *page 97*

Read through the information box, *Organizing Main Ideas*, together with your students. Remind students that it is not always a clear, black-and-white issue to identify the strongest argument. An argument's strength rests on many factors, including the reader's likely response and how much supporting information the writer can give. Additionally, some students may feel that their main ideas can be ordered more persuasively in an order other than emphatic order.

While it is beyond the scope of this book to explore all of the possibilities, allow students to think through the options. While many options are possible, one not uncommon alternative to emphatic ordering is reverse-emphatic, where the strongest argument comes first. This is especially useful when the writer's argument rests primarily on one dominant point. Sandwich order is also sometimes popular, where a strong point opens, followed by a weak point, and ending with a strong point. Sandwich order may be effective when a writer has two strong points and one weak point.

D Add counterarguments *page 98*

Read through the information box, *Double Lists*, with your students. As a class, discuss a scenario where a teenager wants to go out late to a concert with friends, but must first persuade her parents to let her go. List the teen's arguments, and the parents' likely counterarguments, on the board.

Practice 4 *pages 98–99*

As a class, discuss students' completion of this chart.

Answers

Essay title: Fast Food Is Bad for You

Arguments against my opinion	Arguments for my opinion
• most fast-food places offer salads as a choice	• can cause expensive medical problems
• convenient	• most fast food is very high in calories
• cheap	
• salty food tastes good	• salt raises blood pressure
	• easy to eat too often

Your turn *page 99*

You may additionally have students circulate their papers so that two or more classmates can add different counterarguments. This will help to broaden students' perspectives on readers' likely responses.

E Use argumentative language *page 99*

Read through the information box, *Language for Introducing Counterarguments*, with your students. As a class, generate two or three more common phrases that may be used to introduce counterarguments. (For example: *I recently read an article that argued X, but . . . A popular saying says that haste makes waste, but . . .*)

Practice 5 *page 100*

After students have written their sentences, have them share them with a classmate.

Possible answers

2 Some people believe that riding the bus can save money. However, it must also be recognized that time is money, and taking the bus usually takes much longer.

3 Although many people claim that private gun ownership keeps us safe because guns may deter criminals from entering homes, one can also argue that guns are too dangerous for private citizens to keep in their homes because of the possibility of accidents.

4 While it is true that plastic is bad for the environment, some newer plastics are readily biodegradable.

5 Change can be very difficult and stressful, yet if we don't make changes in our lives, our lives will be very boring.

6 While studying overseas is expensive, it gives invaluable exposure to another culture.

Your turn *page 100*

Have students work in pairs to review each other's sentences. A common problem with first-time writers of this type of sentence is that the argument and its counterargument do not really pair. For example, *While some people think that it's not fun to swim on rainy days, I like swimming in the lake.* This could be improved: *While some people think that it's not fun to swim in the lake on rainy days, I like swimming in the lake when it rains.*

F Choose support *page 101*

Read through the information box, *Types of Support*, with your students. Talk about where you would be likely to find these different types of support. For example, you would be likely to find personal experience in a personal essay. In a newspaper article, you might expect to find more expert opinion.

Practice 6 *page 101*

This activity may be done individually or with a partner.

Answers

2	d	5	e
3	f	6	c
4	b	7	g

G Make a detailed outline *page 102*

Remind students that outlining is rarely a linear process, because it constantly generates new ideas and new associations. Encourage students to change their minds, cross out, draw arrows, and so on, as they draft their outline.

H Write the first draft *page 102*

Remind students that they are just drafting their essays. While their brainstorm and outlines have surely stimulated their thinking, and can offer an excellent resource as they draft, students are not obliged to follow their outlines or to stick to their earlier ideas. They are free to write according to their thoughts.

III REVISING YOUR WRITING

A Add support *page 103*

Read through the information box, *The Right Support*, with your students. Have students offer some observations about your school. For example, *More girls take calculus than boys.* Then consider what type of support would be needed to support each of these ideas.

Practice 7 *pages 103–104*

Before doing this activity, students should read through the entire essay. Next, they should read through the five statements of support that they will add to the essay. Finally, they should focus on one support statement at a time, rereading the entire essay to determine its best location.

Answers

a after sentence 9
b after sentence 3
c after sentence 10
d after sentence 2
e after sentence 8

B Benefit from peer feedback *page 105*

Circulate around the room during this activity and make sure that students' responses are complete and clear. Make sure students have adequate time to read and review their partners' essays, and also sufficient time to meet with each other to go over the feedback forms.

C Improve the conclusion *page 106*

Read through the information box, *Concluding Statements*, with your students. Talk about why a concluding statement should be powerful.

Practice 8 *page 106*

After students have discussed their answers, take a quick vote to see how the majority weighed in on this issue. Discuss their reasons.

Answers will vary.

Your turn *page 107*

Encourage students to write concluding statements of different types, such as one question, one quote, and one prediction.

D Make revision decisions *page 107*

Have students use a different color pen to mark changes on their paper. This may help them see how much they are changing. Although students may focus on changes recommended by their peers, remind them that they may want to make changes of their own, too.

E Write the second draft *page 107*

Encourage students to try to limit themselves to revising the content and organization of their second draft, as changing such major elements in a third draft can be tricky.

EDITING YOUR WRITING

A Edit for modals *page 107*

Read through the information box, *Modals and Modal Alternatives*, with your students. Point out that modal alternatives are precisely that – alternatives. They offer variety, especially when a given essay includes a lot of modals.

Practice 9 *pages 107–108*

Answers

Good dental care will keep your teeth healthy and attractive. First, you should eat right. You ~~don't should~~ *shouldn't* eat too many foods that are high in sugar. Next, you must care for your teeth well. Ideally, you should ~~to~~ brush your teeth after each meal. However, often this is not practical. At a minimum, you ought *to* brush twice a day: morning and night. In addition to brushing, you should floss your teeth once a day. You must floss in order to clean between the teeth and to keep your gums healthy. When you floss, you must ~~to~~ be careful to floss deep at the gum line. Finally, you should ~~to~~ have regular checkups at the dentist's. In these ways, you can keep your teeth healthy and your smile bright for years to come.

Practice 10 *page 108*

Answers

Even though the raising of children is not an easy job or a traditional job for Japanese men, we <u>must</u> accept that it is partly men's work, too. Japanese fathers <u>ought to</u> help more in the home. After all, the children are theirs, too. Also, the Japanese government and companies <u>should</u> set up a better system of parental leave so that both parents <u>can</u> care for their families. My brother-in-law, for example, didn't take his paternal leave because he thought it <u>would</u> hurt his career. I have heard many similar stories. Taking paternal leave <u>should</u> not threaten a man's job security. In Norway, for instance, men <u>can</u> and do take paternity leave without concern for their careers. Perhaps Japanese companies <u>should</u> consider making paternity leave a requirement so that there <u>can</u> be no question about its impact on one's career. Paternity leave is important because it helps families to understand the father's role sooner, when babies are young.

Modal changes for variety:

Japanese fathers <u>ought to</u> help more in the home. → <u>It is essential that</u> Japanese fathers help more in the home.

Taking paternal leave should not threaten a man's job security. → <u>It is important that</u> fathers be able to take paternal leave without threatening their jobs.

Practice 11 *page 108*

Possible answers

> Good dental care will keep your teeth healthy and attractive. First, ~~you should~~ *it is essential that you* eat right. You shouldn't eat too many foods that are high in sugar. Next, *it is important to* ~~you must~~ care for your teeth well. Ideally, you should brush your teeth after each meal. However, often this is not practical. At a minimum, ~~you ought~~ *it is necessary* to brush twice a day: morning and night. In addition to brushing, you should floss your teeth once a day. *It is important to* ~~You must~~ floss in order to clean between the teeth and to keep your gums healthy. When you floss, you must be careful to floss deep *it is essential to* at the gum line. Finally, ~~you should~~ have regular checkups at the dentist's. In these ways, you can keep your teeth healthy and your smile bright for years to come.

Your turn *page 108*

Encourage students to count their modals as they read, and to keep a running tally. This will give them a concrete reference for their use of modals. They may tally according to modal, such as "should = 4," as people tend to use the same words over and over.

B Benefit from peer editing *page 109*

Read through the information box, *Peer Feedback*, with your students. Have students limit their editorial input to a circle with a question mark.

C Write the final draft *page 109*

Final drafts can be assigned as homework.

V FOLLOWING UP

A Share your writing *page 109*

For this activity, it may be best for students to read essays they have not read before.

B Check your progress *page 110*

Students can complete the *Progress Check* in class or as homework. If time allows, meet with students individually to go over the *Progress Check*.

Responding to a Reading

In Chapter 5, students will read a published opinion essay and then a student's essay in reaction to it. They will then choose a different opinion article to respond to; consider whether they wish to respond directly to the article or to the article's topic, using the article as support; and decide how to write an appropriate thesis statement. Students will learn when and how to cite information from an article, both as paraphrased information and direct quotes. They will review and add to information in previous chapters about avoiding overgeneralizations, learn and classify a variety of reporting verbs, and check their essays to ensure a variety of sentence structures.

With your students, read the chapter introduction on page 111. Ask, *Where are some places that you read opinion essays and articles? What opinions have you read recently? Did you agree or disagree with them?*

GETTING STARTED

A Think about the sample essay topic *page 112*

Explain to students that they will read a student's response to an essay about concerns over Internet privacy. Before students look at the chart, ask them to brainstorm as a class some reasons that people are worried about having their personal information accessed online. If students do not bring up the idea of identity theft on their own, briefly explain what it is and ask students how they think identity theft occurs. Then go over the chart briefly with the whole class to make sure students understand all of the vocabulary and what the chart shows (top sources of identity theft in the United States in the year 2006). Then have students answer the questions in a small group. If you like, ask one student in each group to take notes and to be responsible for sharing some of the group's answers with the whole class.

Answers

1 from a lost or stolen wallet, credit card, or checkbook
2–5 Answers will vary.

B Read the sample essay *pages 113–114*

Before students read the student essay, have them read the magazine article "The End of Privacy" on pages 159–161. This is an adaptation of a longer article that originally appeared in *Forbes* magazine. If students are interested in reading the entire article, they can visit the author's Web site at www.penenberg.com/ story_archive.html. To help students with their comprehension of the article as it appears in the appendix of the Student's book, use the photocopiable worksheet on page 73 of this teacher's manual. Students can answer the questions individually or in pairs.

After students have read and discussed the article, have them read the sample essay. Ask students to think about the focus question as they read the essay.

C Notice the essay structure *page 114*

Read through the information box, *Response Essays*, with your students. Point out that students are often asked to respond to articles that contain a strong opinion. They will therefore need to identify the writer's opinion and formulate their own opinion, and accurately convey both in their response essay.

Practice 1 *page 114*

Have students work through Practice 1 with a partner, or first answer the questions individually and then compare answers with classmates.

Answers

1 using Penenberg's evidence to support his own ideas
2 *Easy access to personal information is a serious and growing problem.* (Students may feel that the next sentence is part of the thesis as well: *We need to tighten security so that people can enjoy the benefits that technology brings*).
3 problem / solution
4 in the first paragraph (the introduction)
5 five pieces of information, of which two are direct quotes
6 The student writer agrees that Internet privacy is a problem. However, he believes that being careful can keep one safe to enjoy the convenience of the Internet.
7 Answers will vary.

D Select an article *page 115*

Give students time in class to skim the two articles in the appendix, "Don't Shoot: Why Video Games Are Really Linked to Violence" and "Kids May Be Right After All: Homework Stinks." Encourage them to choose the topic that is more interesting to them, but be aware that "Kids May Be Right After All" is a shorter and simpler essay. Remind students that they do not need to agree with the writer of the essay. When students have made their selection, have them tell you and keep a list, so that you can group students more easily for further discussions in this chapter.

E Brainstorm *page 115*

Read through the information box, *Using Discussions to Brainstorm*, with your students. Point out that students do not need to agree with one another while they are talking, but that they should listen carefully to all ideas that come up. They should discuss with a pencil in hand so that they can easily take notes.

Practice 2 *page 115*

Circulate while students are discussing to help out as needed. Make sure students are taking notes that will help them as they brainstorm ideas for their essay. If some students are not discussing much, move them to a smaller group or have them work in pairs.

Answers will vary.

Your turn *page 116*

Students can brainstorm with others who have chosen the same article, or brainstorm on their own.

II PREPARING THE FIRST DRAFT

A Compose the thesis statement *page 116*

Read through the information box, *Stating Your Position*, with your students. It is important that they understand that even a response essay is still an essay whose thesis states their own position – either a position on the topic, or a position on the article to which they're responding.

Practice 3 *pages 116–117*

Answers

1 c
2 a
3 b

Your turn *page 117*

Have students share their thesis statements in small groups, if possible with others who are writing about the same article. Circulate while students are talking to check thesis statements yourself.

B Make an outline *page 117*

Remind students to look back at their brainstormed ideas and thesis statement as they fill in their outline – and that a more complete outline means an easier time writing their essay.

C Write your introduction *page 118*

Show students how they can check the main points in their outline to make sure that they are all previewed in a sentence in the introduction that shows scope.

D Critical thinking *page 118*

Read through the information box, *Choosing Support from an Article*, with your students. Explain that because they will be choosing only a few pieces of support for an essay of the length they are writing for this assignment, it is critical that they choose the strongest pieces of support possible from the article. Deciding when to paraphrase and when to quote directly can be difficult, and it takes practice. Students should be prepared to question and defend their choices in discussions with classmates and with you. Some students choose – disastrously – to quote those sentences in the article that they do not fully understand. Insist that students know the meaning of any excerpt from the article that they wish to paraphrase or quote!

Practice 4 *pages 118–119*

Answers will vary. Make sure students who have made different choices explain their reasoning to their partners. If time allows, have students share their ideas with the whole class after their group discussion is finished.

Your turn *page 119*

Remind students that they are choosing information that will support the thesis of their essays, and also that they should be sure that they completely understand the information they underline.

E Paraphrase an author's opinions *page 120*

Read through the information box, *Paraphrasing*, with your students. Because many students attempt to paraphrase simply by finding synonyms for key nouns and verbs, point out that this is usually the least successful strategy. Instead, students should begin by changing the syntax and grammar of the original sentence. Students can practice paraphrasing by covering up the original text and explaining it to a partner.

Practice 5 *pages 120–121*

After students have finished, go over the wrong answers with the class, and help them to see which poor paraphrases are a result of too literal an interpretation and which are the result of merely substituting synonyms for some key words. Emphasize that it is possible to paraphrase correctly in more than one way.

Answers

1 b and c are acceptable
2 a and b are acceptable
3 a and c are acceptable

F Cite an article *page 121*

Read through the information box, *Citing an Article*, with your students. Explain that because different academic fields have different citing conventions, students need not memorize the MLA rules. Rather, they should be learning how to copy from a given example, and how to integrate quotations into entire sentences. More complete information on this style of citations can be found in the *MLA Handbook* and on various Internet sites.

Practice 6 *pages 121–122*

Possible answers

1 As Penenberg explains, this type of information used to be stored in large centralized computers not accessible to most individuals (159).
2 These days, however, people's privacy is at a higher risk because of more sophisticated search engines and the existence of databases that store personal information (Penenberg 159).
3 Penenberg feels it's unlikely that Congress will pass a bill to make pretext calling illegal, since it has already failed to pass over 100 such bills in the past two years (161).
4 Schaffer suggests that people who play violent video games were already violent people before they started playing games, and that that is why they choose to play such games (162).
5 One problem with playing violent video games, as Schaffer points out, is that players can get used to seeing violence and therefore won't be as bothered by it in real life (163).
6 Kohn argues that there aren't any studies that have proven that doing homework helps children (164–165).
7 No one has ever proven that children will be harmed if they do less or even no homework (Kohn 165).

G Quote an author *page 122*

Read through the information box, *Quoting*, with your students. Again, stress that students should never include a quotation that they do not completely understand. If you like, have students go back to the Penenberg article on pages 159–161 and see the places in which Penenberg chose to quote outside sources. Discuss with students why Penenberg might have chosen to quote directly in those cases instead of paraphrasing.

Practice **7** *page 123*

Possible answers

1 Penenberg claims that the situation is "far worse" than most people know (159).
2 According to Penenberg, people have "willingly given up some privacy in exchange for convenience" (159).
3 Penenberg points out how easy it is to order someone else's personal information online, comparing it to online shopping. "You click through it and load up an online shopping cart as casually as if you were at Amazon.com," he explains (160).
4 However, what Cohn does is "not illegal," according to Penenberg (160).
5 Cohn was able to find out a great deal of personal information about Penenberg's bank account, including, as he explains, "my account balance, direct deposits from work, withdrawals, ATM visits, check numbers with dates and amounts, and the name of my broker" (160).

Your turn *page 123*

If students found paraphrasing and quoting difficult, have them write out their paraphrases and quotes fully before they start the rough draft. They can check them in groups or have you check them.

H Write the first draft *page 123*

Students can write their rough drafts in class or as homework. If they write in class, circulate while they are working to answer questions about organization, quoting, and paraphrasing.

III REVISING YOUR WRITING

A Benefit from peer feedback *page 124*

Make sure students have adequate time (at least 20 minutes) to read and process their partners' essays, and also sufficient time to meet with each other to go over the feedback forms (about 10 minutes). You may want to have students who chose the same article work together, but it is not necessary; their explanation of the topic should be clear enough for a reader who has not read the original article to understand it.

B Check for generalizations *page 125*

Read through the information box, *Revising Generalizations with Hedging*, with your students. If necessary, review the information in Chapter 2 on page 160. Also point out that using too many hedging devices can make writing seem weak; students should be thinking about each sentence and how sure they are about their claims, and then choosing language accordingly.

Practice 8 *page 125*

Possible answer

> _{can be}
> It is dangerous to use the Internet for shopping. Sites _{often} always ask for credit
> card _{some} information and all of your other personal information such as your
> address and telephone number. _{Occassionally,} Computer experts "hack," or illegally break into,
> companies' Web sites and _{could} steal their customers' information. Then customers
> _{might} not only lose _{some of} all their money but risk identify theft. I know _{a few} people who have had
> problems _{some} with information stolen in this way. Companies should collect personal
> information over the phone, not on their Web sites.

Your turn *page 125*

If they are comfortable doing so, students can also exchange essays with a partner and check each other's essays for possible overgeneralizations. However, caution students not to make their sentences overly weak, either.

C Use a variety of reporting verbs *page 126*

Read through the information box, *Reporting Verbs*, with your students. There are hundreds of possibilities for reporting verbs, but these are some of the most common. Encourage students to use a variety of them and not to depend just on a few. While many words in English are similar, no two words mean exactly the same thing, so students should be sensitive to differences in shades of meaning.

Practice 9 *page 126*

When they have finished the exercise, ask students if they feel the author used enough different reporting verbs. Are there any places where they could suggest changes?

Possible answer

First paragraph: points out
Second paragraph: reports
Third paragraph: explains
Fourth paragraph: advises
Fifth paragraph: (none)

Possible answer

>   High school students these days ~~say~~ *complain* they have too much homework. They
> ~~say~~ *claim* they don't have enough time for other activities, such as sports and
> music, because they are too busy. Many parents ~~say the same~~ *agree*. They ~~say~~ *describe* their
> children don't get enough sleep and are even skipping meals. Some teachers,
> however, ~~say~~ *assert* that homework is essential for students. In fact, recent studies
> ~~say that~~ *prove* most teachers assign only two to three hours of homework per week.
> Some teachers ~~say~~ *maintain that* students are too busy because they do too many outside
> activities or do not know how to budget their time wisely.

Your turn *page 127*

Circulate while students are working to help with vocabulary. If students want to use their dictionaries to find other reporting verbs, ask them to check with you or another native speaker to make sure that the verbs have the intended shade of meaning.

D Write a bibliography *page 127*

Read through the information box, *Citing an Article*, with your students. As with in-text citations, this book does not attempt to cover all kinds of bibliographic entries, just those relevant to the articles in the appendix about which students will be writing. Students should copy the format given in the book, and not try to memorize the patterns. (Note that to help students practice citations, we are asking them to pretend in a sense that they are accessing the original source, not reading the article in a textbook.)

Practice **11** *page 127*

When students have finished, go over the answers with the whole class, and write the correct format on the board. Make sure that every student has the answers written correctly. Remind them that they will need the bibliography entry for their essays.

Answers

1 Schaffer, Amanda. "Don't Shoot: Why Video Games Really Are Linked to Violence." Slate (27 April 2007). 15 July 2007 <http://www.slate.com/id/2164065>.

2 Kohn, Alfie. "Kids May Be Right After All: Homework Stinks." USA Today (14 September 2006). 15 July 2007 <http://www.alfiekohn.org/teaching/kmbraa.htm>.

E Make revision decisions *page 127*

Remind the class that each student must make his or her own decisions about using the suggestions given during peer feedback.

F Write the second draft *page 127*

Students can write the second draft in class or as homework.

IV EDITING YOUR WRITING

A Check for variety of sentences *page 128*

Read through the information box, *Sentence Variety*, with your students. Explain that varying sentence types is the mark of a high-level writer. The more they practice this skill, the easier it will become.

Practice 12 *pages 128–129*

Possible answers

> Answers will vary. However, Paragraph A has the most sentence variety. Students should point out differences such as the opening question and the sentences that begin with a subordinating clause.

Practice 13 *page 129*

Answers

> Although credit cards are convenient
> not only
> but also
> More expensive than
> If you don't want
> consider using

Your turn *page 129*

If students complete this in class, circulate while they are working to help out with offering alternate sentence structures.

B Edit for punctuation *page 130*

Read through the information box, *Using quotation marks, commas, and periods,* with your students. These rules are specific to MLA style, and there is no reason for students to memorize them. Remind students that style guides exist for different documentation systems and that these guides give all of the punctuation rules. Writers of essays and research papers consult the appropriate style guide for the type of paper they are writing and then copy the formatting exactly. Students will be practicing this skill as they follow the examples in the information box on page 130 while they complete Practice 14.

Practice 14 *page 130*

Answers

1 "Computers now hold half a billion bank accounts," reports Penenberg (page 159).
2 Penenberg poses the question, "Why should we care if our personal information isn't so personal anymore?" (page 159).
3 Penenberg explains, "Docusearch's clients include lawyers, insurers, private detectives, and businesses" (page 160).
4 "Docusearch's clients include lawyers, insurers, private detectives, and businesses," explains Penenberg (page 160).
5 Penenberg claims that Cohn got the author's bank account number "directly from the source" (page 160).

Your turn *page 130*

If they are comfortable doing so, students can also exchange essays with a partner and check each other's essays for punctuation.

C Write the final draft *page 131*

Make sure students know when their final drafts are due. Ask them to attach their first drafts to the bottom of the final drafts so that you can see their progress. You may also ask them to attach their brainstorming notes.

V FOLLOWING UP

A Share your writing *page 131*

As far as possible, have students work in groups with others who wrote on the same essay. Keep groups to three or four students.

B Check your progress *page 131*

Students can complete the *Progress Check* in class or as homework. You could even ask students to e-mail their *Progress Checks* to you. Students can look back at their *Progress Checks* from previous chapters.

Chapter 6 — Timed Essays

For Chapter 6, students will think about some of the common tests and testing situations they may encounter. They will read a sample timed essay written by a student and examine some of its standard features. They will compare the processes of writing untimed and timed essays, practicing each step by writing the various pieces of an essay under a time limit. Students will consider the opportunities for editing and revision of timed work. They will look at some useful transition words and ways to avoid run-on sentences. Students will study ways to manage stress. Finally, they will write an entire timed essay.

With your students, read the chapter introduction on page 133. Encourage students to share their experiences with high-stakes, timed writing. For example, have any of your students, or their family members, ever needed to write an essay in order to get a job?

I GETTING STARTED

A Think about timed essays *page 134*

To open the topic of timed writings on standardized exams, talk about a specific exam that may affect many students in your class. Then look at the chart on page 134. Read aloud the name of each test, so that students can pronounce it confidently. Then have students discuss the chart and the questions that follow.

B Read the sample timed essay *page 135*

Read or have a student read aloud the focus questions. Before students read the essay, have them read and talk about the test question. Next, have students read the student's essay, "Grades Motivate Students." After they finish reading, have them briefly discuss the focus questions with a partner.

C Notice features of a timed essay *page 136*

Read through the information box, *Timed Essays*, with your students. Ask students to think about times and situations in the past when their writing has been graded. Write their ideas on the board.

Practice 1 *pages 136–137*

Possible answers

1 Grades encourage students for several reasons. They help students see their learning progress, reward students, and show a student's position compared to classmates.

2 The introduction states the writer's thesis and shows the scope of the essay by introducing the main ideas.

3 First, grades help students see their progress in learning, because grades reflect students' efforts in class.
In addition to inspiring them to work harder, grades may help students to find interest in a subject.
Most importantly, students like to know that their work is recognized. Yes, each topic is mentioned in the introduction. Also, each topic is well supported.

4 Transition words: first, in addition, most importantly. Yes, the organization is logical, though many other organizations would also be effective.

5 It is short, and this may be OK in a timed essay.

6 There is a good variety of sentence types, and the vocabulary and grammar are appropriate.

7 Yes.

8 Yes. It is a good idea so that the person grading the essay can make editorial marks.

D Follow the writing process *page 137*

Read through the information box, *The Writing Process for a Timed Essay*, with your students. Ask students if they know of other differences in the writing process between a timed and untimed essay. Discuss their answers.

Practice 2 *pages 137–138*

Answers

1 b	3 c	5 b	7 a
2 c	4 b	6 c	8 c

Practice 3 *page 138*

Go over students' answers orally, writing on the board the times suggested for each writing step. Have students explain their reasons for the amount of time for each step.

Answers will vary.

Practice 4 *page 139*

Answers

| 1 b   2 a   3 b

E Select a question *page 139*

For the purposes of this essay, students should choose one of the listed topics, rather than creating their own. This has the additional benefit of simulating an actual timed essay situation, where students rarely have the option of selecting their own topic. Make sure that students understand that their topic selection will be the topic of their writing over the next several activities in this book. Also, be aware that while this essay assignment would ideally be completed in 30 minutes, the writing in this chapter is broken down into individual steps. Invariably, this start-and-stop method may add a few minutes to the total writing time.

II WRITING A TIMED ESSAY

A Understand the test question *page 140*

Read through the information box, *Understanding the Test Question*, with your students. Ask students to share other ways that they work to understand a test question. Encourage students to consider what could happen to their essay score if they don't understand the question. How would a student grade an essay that didn't answer the question, compared to one that did?

Practice 5 *page 140*

After doing the matching, encourage students to think of other common terms that they see in test questions. Talk about the meaning of those terms.

Answers

| 1 c   2 f   3 a   4 b   5 d   6 e

Practice 6 *page 141*

Possible answers

1 <u>Explain</u> <u>three</u> ways in which <u>human activities</u> are <u>changing the environment</u>. (a)
2 <u>Consider</u> <u>two ways</u> to lose weight: <u>reducing calories</u> or <u>increasing exercise</u>. <u>Which</u> is a <u>more effective</u> way to lose weight, and <u>why</u>? (a)
3 <u>Discuss</u> <u>two</u> major <u>challenges for students today</u> that students probably did <u>not face 50 years ago</u>. (b)
4 <u>Read</u> the following article about new ways to break the habit of cigarette smoking. Based on this reading, <u>persuade smokers</u> that they should <u>try quitting because</u> it has gotten <u>easier</u>. (b)

Your turn *page 141*

After students have rewritten the question in their own words, have them compare their sentences in groups. Group students according to the question they are answering.

Answers will vary.

B Write a rough outline *page 141*

Read through the information box, *Outlining Quickly*, with your students. Ask students if they write quick outlines before starting timed essays and discuss their answers. Make sure students understand that these outlines are meant to be a way of ordering their ideas and seeing that they have included all main ideas, but require few details.

Practice 7 *page 142*

Possible answer

Answers may vary. However, Outline A is better in many key ways: it's shorter, and the body paragraphs relate directly to the thesis statement. It could be improved by adding more support to each paragraph. Outline B would take too long to write.

Practice 8 *page 143*

For each essay question, time students while they write for five minutes. Then have them stop, and go to the next question, again timing while they write. Once they have finished the three questions, students can compare outlines in pairs or in small groups.

Answers will vary.

Your turn *page 143*

Use a timer, if available, or a clock or watch to time the class. After they have written their questions, give them three minutes to brainstorm ideas, then five minutes to write their outlines. Make sure that students stop when the time is up, even if they are not finished. At this point, they are both practicing writing their responses and getting a feel for timing. Students can check their own outlines from the gray box on page 141, or can work with a partner and check each other's work.

C Write an introduction *page 143*

Read through the information box, *Timed Essay Introductions*, with your students. As a class, discuss the ideas in the information. Ask students if they agree or disagree, and encourage them to add additional thoughts to the discussion.

Practice 9 *page 144*

Possible answer

Answers will vary. In general, Introductions 2 and 4 may score high. They are both short, their amount of background is appropriate, and they prepare readers well

66 Chapter 6

for the essay. Introduction 3 is weak, since it has no hook, offers no background, states no thesis (or, if it has a thesis, it is much too broad), and gives random information about the writer's school. Introduction 1 is the weakest, since it is too long, it has no hook, it doesn't prepare the reader, and the thesis is unclear. Is the essay about Peru's inefficient educational system, or study opportunities in the United States?

Your turn *page 144*

Remind students, for the sake of practice, to write neatly and to double-space their work.

D Write the body *page 145*

Read through the information box, *Choosing Support*, with your students. If you think students may benefit from a review, go to Chapter 4, page 101.

Practice 10 *pages 145–146*

This activity could be assigned as homework. As a class, review several students' answers for each paragraph. Have students identify what kind of support has been added.

Answers will vary.

Your turn *page 146*

Have students review their support before they start writing their body paragraphs. Remind them that testing rarely allows for content-level revision, so that in a timed-writing situation, the writer should plan all of his or her major points of support before writing.

E Write a conclusion *page 146*

Read through the information box, *Timed-Essay Conclusions*, with your students. Encourage students to share their own experiences or thoughts in writing the conclusion for a timed essay.

Practice 11 *page 147*

Possible answers

Answers will vary. In general, Conclusion 1 is short and to the point. Conclusion 2 is too long and too detailed, apparently trying to summarize the whole essay. Conclusions 3 and 4 are strong and witty, but could be quite difficult to write in a limited period of time.

Your turn *page 147*

Time students as they write for five minutes. Do not give students extra time.

A Revise ideas *page 148*

Read through the information box, *Making Content Changes*, with your students.
Discuss these topics related to the first bulleted point: *What type of content is
necessary for an essay? What content makes a major contribution? What would be
considered minor content?*

Practice 12 *page 148*

Answers

> Playing violent video games has a dangerous effect on young players. These
> games may encourage the negative emotions of children who already feel
> angry or isolated. ~~Although most young players are boys, many girls also play
> video games on a regular basis.~~ In video games, it is acceptable to be violent
> *As young people play these games, they may lose touch with the real consequences of real violence.*
> and angry. It is OK to use a gun and shoot many people. Even being shot is
> perfectly fine because players are brought back to life with the click of a button.
> Young players may think that violence is an acceptable solution in the real
> world.

B Connect ideas *page 149*

Read through the information box, *Transitions*, with your students. Put an example
on the board of two sentences. *John's mother told him he couldn't go to the movies.
He went to the movies.* Have students connect them with different transition words
(*and, but, so, for*) to show the different meanings and impact.

Practice 13 *page 149*

Answers

2 Usually volcano eruptions follow several earthquakes. <u>For example</u>, in the 24-hour
period before the eruption in May, nine earthquakes were recorded.
3 At many U.S. universities, female students dramatically outnumber males, <u>so</u>
college administrations are considering how to attract more male students.
4 Many students have to decide whether to go to college full-time and take out a
student loan, <u>or</u> go to college part-time and get a job.
5 Dancers develop a sense of balance <u>and</u> they develop a sense of grace.
6 Two of the boys speak Finnish <u>because</u> they study at a Finnish school on the
weekends.

Your turn *page 149*

Time students as they write for five minutes, reminding them when just one
minute remains.

IV EDITING A TIMED ESSAY

A Check for run-on sentences *page 150*

Read the information box, *Fixing Run-Ons*, with your students. At this level, many students are likely aware of what constitutes a reasonable sentence and what would be a run-on. Remind students that while they may not consider themselves likely to produce a lot of run-ons, the pressure of time can cause writing errors that they may not usually make.

Practice 14 *pages 150–151*

Answers

2 Since we live in a large apartment building, I know a lot of other kids who are my age and we can always find something to do.
3 Sometimes I can't answer the teacher's question, even though I know the answer.
4 Members of varsity sports teams aren't supposed to hold part-time jobs, but it's not legal for the school district to forbid them.
5 It's not legal for the school district to forbid them, but it's kind of an unspoken rule.
6 Most of the crossword puzzles in this book are so long, I can't do them all at once. So, I have to go back once or twice, or sometimes even three times, to get all the words.

Practice 15 *page 151*

Possible answers

1 OK
2 RO The agents typically buy inexpensive land at the edge of a town. Then they wait for the population to grow enough that the inexpensive land becomes more attractive. This way they can sell it at a profit.
3 RO Trying to do homework in the library while other people are talking or whispering frustrates students. They end up being inconvenienced by other people's rudeness.
4 OK

Your turn *page 151*

Encourage students to think through and plan their solutions before marking them on their papers. While a run-on sentence is bad, a run-on sentence with multiple fixes and crossed-out fixes is even worse.

B Edit language *page 151*

Read through the information box, *Editing a Timed Essay*, with your students. Make sure that students understand each of the listed items. Talk about how students can identify their own errors. While students will rarely have dictionaries or grammar books available to them during a test, this doesn't mean they cannot improve their own work. Encourage students to follow their intuition about things that seem wrong in their writing.

Practice 16 *page 152*

Answers

My ~~homtown~~ [*hometown*], Guiyu, China, recently become [*has*] the world's biggest electronic garbage dump. The developed world exports its old electronics to Guiyu for reprocessing. In Guiyu, thousands [*of*] family workshops handle this ~~stuff~~ [*waste*]. While this work provide[*s*] them ~~cash~~ [*with an income*], residents pay a ~~different~~ [*different*] price for accepting this industry. The price is their health. ~~Bosses~~ [*Employers*] don't care about workers' health. They ignore laws, releasing toxic fumes into the air and dumping acid into rivers. Guiyu must recognize the environmental and health hazards of its biggest industry. If the town want[*s*] to clean up [*the*] environment and protect the health of its citizen[*s*], it will ~~having~~ [*have*] to strengthen laws for handling waste and punish ~~law-breakers~~ [*violators*].

Your turn *page 152*

Write the errors on the board that students should watch for: spelling, punctuation, missing words, correct verb forms and tense, subject-verb agreement, academic language. Encourage each student to watch for an additional language item that they think they frequently have problems with.

C Add a title *page 152*

Give students about one minute to produce a title.

Practice 17 *page 152*

Possible answers

1 Final Papers Score High
2 Cambodia's Political Exiles
3 Children Choose on Internet

Your turn *page 152*

Have students share their titles with a classmate or small group, if possible with those who have read their essays already. Remind students to capitalize the first word and all content words of their titles.

V TAKING A TEST

A Manage stress *page 153*

Read through the information box, *Managing Stress*, with your students. As a class, brainstorm some ways that students experience stress, such as inability to sleep, distraction, or excess energy. List students' ideas on the board.

Practice 18 *page 154*

Answers will vary.

B Write a timed essay *page 154*

Read through the information box, *Reviewing Essay Timing*, with your students. Remind students that this is just a guide. As a class, calculate the percentages of time that are suggested for each phase – planning, writing, revising and editing. Put students in groups, assigning each group to calculate the same percentages for essays of other common lengths: 20 minutes, 45 minutes, 60 minutes.

Your turn *page 154*

Time students as they write their essays. Let them know when they have 5 minutes remaining. Collect their essays when they are done if they will not be moving on to the self-reflection in the same class period.

C Evaluate your own writing *page 155*

Make sure that students fill in this form. It is not enough for them simply to think about its questions.

D Benefit from peer feedback *page 156*

Encourage students to complete this form without looking at their partner's completion of the self-reflection form.

E Check your progress *page 157*

Students can complete the *Progress Check* in class or as homework. This is a good time for students to look through all of their previous *Progress Checks* and to reflect on their writing.

WORKSHEET

Read the article "The End of Privacy" on pages 159–161. Then answer the questions about the article.

1 Why did Penenberg write this article?
   a. He had lost some of his personal information.
   b. He wanted to prove that people are in danger.
   c. Somebody paid him to find some information.

2 Who is Dan Cohn? What is his job, and what company does he work for? Why did he look for information about Penenberg?

3 How much information did Cohn have about Penenberg when he began his investigation? What kinds of additional information did he discover? How long did it take him?

4 Check (✓) the methods that Cohn used to find information.
   ___ He asked Penenberg to give him information.
   ___ He used the Internet.
   ___ He called Penenberg's employer.
   ___ He called Penenberg's friends and family.
   ___ He called Penenberg's bank and phone company.
   ___ He wrote letters.
   ___ He called Penenberg's broker.
   ___ He hired a licensed state investigator.

5 Did Cohn break any laws?

6 What does Penenberg hope readers will do or believe after they have read his article?
   a. Be more careful with their personal information.
   b. Find out about other people more easily.
   c. Stop using the Internet.

7 Check (✓) the statements that Penenberg would probably agree with.
   ___ Using the Internet is convenient.
   ___ Businesses ask for more personal information than they really need.
   ___ Average citizens are at risk.
   ___ Only people who are rich or have secrets need to be worried that someone will find out their information.
   ___ There should be more laws to protect consumers.
   ___ People cannot do anything to protect themselves.
   ___ Companies like Cohn's should be illegal.
   ___ Most people already know about this problem.

8 Put a star (*) by the statements in 7 that you agree with.

Answers to the worksheet on page 73 of this Teacher's Manual.

1 b

2 Dan Cohn is an Internet detective. He works for Docusearch, a Web detective agency in Florida. He looked for information about Penenberg because Penenberg issued him a challenge.

3 Cohn had only Penenberg's first name, last name, and middle initial when he began his investigation. He discovered Penenberg's middle name, birth date, address, Social Security number, salary, phone numbers, records of his phone calls, and information abut his bank account: account balance, direct deposits from work, withdrawals, ATM visits, check numbers with dates and amounts, and the name of his broker. It took him six days.

4 He used the Internet.
   He called Penenberg's bank and phone company.

5 No, Cohn didn't break any laws.

6 a

7 Using the Internet is convenient.
   Businesses ask for more personal information than they really need.
   Average citizens are at risk.
   There should be more laws to protect consumers.
   Companies like Cohn's should be illegal.

8 Answers will vary.

CPSIA information can be obtained at www.ICGtesting.com
Printed in the USA
LVOW09s1216121215

466417LV00002B/19/P